as main map
SHETLAND ISLANDS (Br.)
YELL
St. Magnus Bay
MAINLAND
Lerwick
FOULA
SUMBURGH HD.
FAIR ISLAND
N. RONALDSAY
SANDAY
STRONSAY
Kirkwall
MAINLAND
ORKNEY ISLANDS (Br.)
S. RONALDSAY
DUNCANSBY HD.
©RMCN.
HOY
S. RONALDSAY
Pentland Firth
DUNCANSBY HD
CAPE WRATH
BUTT OF LEWIS
Thurso
Wick
Ben Hope 3041
ISLE OF LEWIS
Stornoway
The Minch
Ben More 3274
ST. KILDA
HARRIS
OUTER HEBRIDES
NORTH UIST
SOUTH UIST
Dornoch
Dornoch Firth
Ben Dearg 3547
Dingwall
Moray Firth
KINNAIRDS HD.
Fraserburgh
Elgin
Buckie
Banff
Peterhead
Nairn
Inverness
ISLAND OF SKYE
INNER
Little Minch
Ben Attow 3386
Ben Macdui 4295
Ballater
Aberdeen
Sea of The Hebrides
RHUM
HEBRIDES
Mallaig
S C O T L A N D
Stonehaven
Fort William
Ben Nevis 4406
GRAMPIAN MTS.
COLL
TIREE
ISLAND OF MULL
Forfar
Montrose
Dundee
Arbroath
Oban
Firth of Lorn
Perth
St. Andrews
FIFE NESS
COLONSAY
Buckhaven
Kirkcaldy
Dunfermline
Stirling
Firth of Forth
Helensburgh
Dumbarton
Falkirk
Greenock
Edinburgh
Rothesay
Paisley
GLASGOW
Motherwell
ISLAY
JURA
KINTYRE
Kilmarnock
Lanark
Peebles
Galashiels
Berwick-upon-Tweed
HOLY ISLAND
FARNE IS.
MALIN HD
Campbelltown
RATHLIN ISLAND
ISLAND OF ARRAN
Irvine
Ayr
Hawick
Carndonagh
Girvan
ARAN ISLAND
Errigal 2466
Coleraine
Londonderry
North Channel
U N I T E D
Strabane
Dumfries
Blyth
Tynemouth
ROSSAN POINT
Donegal
N O R T H E R N
ULSTER
Omagh
Belfast
Belfast Lough
NEWCASTLE UPON TYNE
South Shields
Stranraer
Luce Bay
Solway Firth
Carlisle
Gateshead
Sunderland
Donegal Bay
Lisburn
Newtownards
I R E L A N D
Durham
Hartlepool
Killala
Sligo
Enniskillen
Lurgan
Strangford Lough
Workington
Whitehaven
Stockton
Middlesbrough
Ballina
ST. BEES HD
Armagh
Monaghan
MOURNE MTS.
Dundrum Bay
ISLE OF MAN (Br.)
Ramsey
LAKE DISTRICT
Windermere
Kendal
PENNINES
Darlington
Northallerton
NORTH YORK MOORS
ACHILL ISLAND
CLARE ISLAND
Boyle
Castlebar
Westport
Cavan
Barrow-in-Furness
Douglas
Scarborough
CONNACHT
Dundalk
Dundalk Bay
Lancaster
YORKSHIRE WOLDS
Bridlington
Clifden
CONNEMARA
Claremorris
Longford
I R I S H
Blackburn
Burnley
Halifax
Bradford
York
Kingston upon Hull
Drogheda
Blackpool
Preston
LEEDS
Beverley
SLYNE HEAD
Athlone
Mullingar
S E A
Rochdale
Wakefield
Hull
Galway
Ballinasloe
Southport
Bolton
Huddersfield
Galway Bay
Dublin
Wigan
Oldham
Doncaster
Grimsby
(Baile Atha Cliath)
LIVERPOOL
MANCHESTER
Sheffield
Louth
ARAN IS.
Tullamore
Kildare
Dun Laoghaire
Holyhead
HOLY ISLAND
ANGLESEY
Llandudno
Birkenhead
I R E L A N D
Bray
Denbigh
Stockport
UNCOLNSHIRE WOLDS
Bangor
Caernarfon
Chester
Crewe
Lincoln
Chesterfield
Ennis
Nenagh
Athy
Lugnaquilla Mtn. 3039
WICKLOW MTS.
Wicklow
Caernarfon Bay
Snowdon 3560
Ffestiniog
Wrexham
Stoke-on-Trent
The Wash
LOOP HEAD
Kilrush
Carlow
Arklow
Nottingham
Shannon
Limerick
Thurles
LEINSTER
BARDSEY ISLAND
Stafford
Burton
Derby
Grantham
Brandon Mtn. 3127
MUNSTER
Tipperary
Kilkenny
Welshpool
Shrewsbury
Leicester
King's Lynn
GREAT BLASKET ISLAND
Dingle
Tralee
GALTY MTS.
Clonmel
Carrick-on-Suir
New Ross
Enniscorthy
Cardigan
Wolverhampton
Walsall
Nuneaton
Norwich
Dingle Bay
Mallow
Wexford
Aberystwyth
Dudley
BIRMINGHAM
Thetford
VALENCIA ISLAND
Killarney
Carrauntoohill 3414
Fermoy
Waterford
Smethwick
Coventry
Peterborough
Cork
Youghal
Dungarvan
CARNSORE PT.
K I N G D O M
Ely
Bury St. Edmunds
Cobh
Youghal Bay
Cardigan
CAMBRIAN MTS.
Worcester
Warwick
Leamington
Stratford-upon-Avon
Northampton
Bantry
Cork Harbour
St. George's Channel
ST. DAVID'S HD
Hereford
Bedford
Cambridge
Ipswich
Bantry Bay
Skibbereen
OLD HEAD OF KINSALE
Clonakilty Bay
Carmarthen
W A L E S
Merthyr Tydfil
Gloucester
Cheltenham
Luton
Colchester
Llanelli
Neath
Abergavenny
COTSWOLD HILLS
Aylesbury
Hertford
St. Albans
Harwich
Oxford
Chelmsford
Pembroke
Aberdare
Rhondda
Newport
High Wycombe
Watford
Brentwood
Swansea
Cardiff
Bristol
Swindon
Reading
Windsor
Southend-on-Sea
Basildon
Thames
Newbury
LONDON
Ilfracombe
Bristol Channel
Weston-super-Mare
Bath
E N G L A N D
Gillingham
Chatham
Canterbury
LUNDY
Barnstaple
EXMOOR
SALISBURY PLAIN
Aldershot
Guildford
Reigate
Maidstone
HARTLAND PT.
Taunton
Yeovil
Salisbury
NORTH DOWNS
Dover
BLACK DOWN HILLS
Tunbridge Wells
Folkestone
Honiton
Winchester
SOUTH DOWNS
THE WEALD
Hastings
Exeter
Dorchester
Poole
Southampton
Chichester
Hove
Lewes
Bexhill
Strait of Dover
Launceston
DARTMOOR
BODMIN MOOR
Bodmin
Exmouth
Weymouth
Cowes
Ryde
Newport
Portsmouth
Brighton
Worthing
Eastbourne
BEACHY HEAD
Boulogne-sur-Mer
Étaples
Plymouth
Torquay (Torbay)
Bournemouth
ISLE OF WIGHT
Truro
Dartmouth
Camborne
START PT.
E N G L I S H
C H A N N E L
Penzance
LAND'S END
Falmouth
LIZARD PT.
ISLES OF SCILLY
St. Valéry-sur-Somme
Le Tréport
A T L A N T I C
O C E A N
N
Relief
Feet
2000
1000
500
0
Below Sea Level
©Rand McNally & Co. R.L. 83-S-141
Longitude West of Greenwich
Scale 1: 4 000 000; one inch to 64 miles. Conic Projection
Elevations and depressions are given in feet
0 10 20 30 40 50 60 70 80 90 100 110 120 Miles
0 20 40 60 80 100 120 140 160 180 200 Kilometers

ATLANTIC
OCEAN
IRISH
SEA
St. George's Channel
Bristol Channel
Cardigan Bay
Donegal Bay
Sligo Bay
Galway Bay
Dingle Bay
Bantry Bay
IRELAND
U.K.
EIRE
ULSTER
CONNAUGHT
LEINSTER
MUNSTER
DONEGAL
MAYO
GALWAY
ROSCOMMON
LEITRIM
CAVAN
MONAGHAN
LONGFORD
MEATH
WESTMEATH
LOUTH
OFFALY
KILDARE
DUBLIN
LAOIGHIS
WICKLOW
CARLOW
KILKENNY
WEXFORD
TIPPERARY
WATERFORD
CLARE
LIMERICK
CORK
KERRY
CONNEMARA
Londonderry
Belfast
Newtownabbey
Carrickfergus
Lisburn
Lurgan
Portadown
Armagh
Newry
Dundalk
Drogheda
Dublin
Baile Átha Cliath
Dun Laoghaire
Bray
Wicklow
Arklow
Gorey
Enniscorthy
Wexford
Rosslare
New Ross
Waterford
Tramore
Dungarvan
Youghal
Cork
Cobh
Midleton
Kinsale
Bandon
Clonakilty
Skibbereen
Baltimore
Bantry
Glengarriff
Kenmare
Killarney
Tralee
Dingle
Listowel
Limerick
Ennis
Kilrush
Kilkee
Galway
Athlone
Tuam
Castlebar
Westport
Ballina
Sligo
Letterkenny
Donegal
Killybegs
Omagh
Enniskillen
Dungannon
Coleraine
Larne
Ballymena
Bangor
Isle of Man
Douglas
Castletown
Ramsey
GLASGOW
Edinburgh
Paisley
Greenock
Motherwell
Hamilton
Kilmarnock
Ayr
Stranraer
Dumfries
Carlisle
Workington
Whitehaven
Barrow-in-Furness
Morecambe
Blackpool
Fleetwood
Southport
Liverpool
Birkenhead
Holyhead
Bangor
Caernarvon
Aberystwyth
Cardigan
Fishguard
Haverfordwest
Milford Haven
Pembroke
Carmarthen
Llanelli
Swansea
Neath
Port Talbot
Merthyr Tydfil
Cardiff
Barry
Weston-super-Mare
Bridgwater
Barnstaple
Ilfracombe
Bideford
Exeter
Torquay (Torbay)
Plymouth
Saint Austell
Truro
Falmouth
Penzance
Land's End
Isles of Scilly
Hugh Town
Lundy

Enchantment of the World

THE REPUBLIC of IRELAND

by Dennis B. Fradin

Consultants: Lawrence J. McCaffrey, Ph.D., Loyola University

Stephen Burke, University of Michigan, Ann Arbor

Consultant for Reading: Robert L. Hillerich, Ph.D., Bowling Green State University, Bowling Green, Ohio

CHILDRENS PRESS, CHICAGO

Dublin schoolchildren

Dedication: For Fran Dyra, her mother came from County Sligo and her father from County Mayo

Library of Congress Cataloging in Publication Data

Fradin, Dennis B.
The Republic of Ireland

(Enchantment of the world)
Includes index.
Summary: Presents a history and description of Ireland, as well as geographical, political, and cultural information.
1. Ireland—Juvenile literature. [1. Ireland]
I. Title. II. Series.
DA906.F72 1984 941.5 83-20960
ISBN 0-516-02767-0 AACR2

Printed in the United States of America.
1 2 3 4 5 6 7 8 9 10 R 93 92 91 90 89 88 87 86 85 84

Picture Acknowledgments
Colour Library International: Cover, pages 5, 9, 10, 12 (2 photos), 13 (right), 16, 68 (bottom right), 70 (2 photos), 75 (bottom), 76 (bottom), 81 (right), 92 (right), 112
Hillstrom Stock Photos
© **Patrick T. Reynolds:** Pages 4, 64 (bottom);
© **David Fraizer:** Pages 71, 82 (right);
© **Margaret Hussey:** Pages 76 (top), 82 (top);
© **Brooks & Vankirk:** Pages 14, 15 (2 photos), 17, 25 (left), 29 (left), 60 (top), 64 (top), 66 (left), 67 (left), 68 (top), 72 (2 photos), 73 (2 photos), 74, 75 (top and middle), 79 (2 photos), 87 (right), 96 (right), 111, 113
Nawrocki Stock Photo/© Jean Clough: Pages 67 (right), 87 (left)
Root Resources
© **Kenneth Radalee:** Pages 6, 66 (right), 81 (left), 94 (right);
© **Evelyn Davidson:** Pages 13 (left), 80;
© **Jane P. Downton:** Pages 60 (bottom), 68 (bottom left)
Joseph A. DiChello, Jr.: Pages 24 (left), 82 (bottom left),
© **Chandler Foreman:** Pages 20, 94 (left), 96 (left)
United Press International: Pages 56 (2 photos), 58 (3 photos), 59 (2 photos), 108
Historical Pictures Service, Inc. Chicago: Pages 23 (2 photos), 24 (right), 25 (right), 26 (2 photos), 28, 29 (right), 31 (3 photos), 33 (2 photos), 35 (2 photos), 40 (2 photos), 43, 45, 46, 47, 48, 49, 100, 101, 103, 105 (2 photos)
Len Meents: Maps pages 9, 10, 52, 71
Courtesy Flag Research Center, Winchester, Massachusetts 01890: Flag on back cover
Cover: Clifden, County Galway

Old-fashioned, thatched-roof cottage in the Kerry Mountains

TABLE OF CONTENTS

Berra Peninsula, County Kerry

Chapter 1

THE EMERALD ISLE

> *The turf is of brighter hue, the hills glow with a richer purple, the varnish of holly and ivy is more glossy. . . I never in my life saw anything more beautiful.*
>
> Thomas Macaulay, nineteenth century English historian, describing Ireland

If on a summer day you could fly over Ireland, you would see why that island is known as the Emerald Isle. The lush meadows are green, as are the pastures filled with grazing livestock. The rolling farmlands resemble a patchwork quilt of various shades of green and yellow. And the tree-covered mountains rise in green and purple grandeur.

Green isn't the only color that brightens the Emerald Isle. Blue ocean waters surround it. Lovely blue rivers and sparkling lakes (or *loughs,* as they are called in Irish) shimmer throughout the green island.

Ireland is less than 100 miles (about 161 kilometers) west of England, and from one spot in Northern Ireland, just 13 miles (21 kilometers) west of Scotland. If you look at a map or globe, you will notice that the island of Ireland contains two separate political parts.

The larger part, called the Republic of Ireland (or the Irish

Republic), occupies 27,136 square miles (70, 282 square kilometers), or about 83 percent of the island. In the northeastern section of the Emerald Isle the smaller part, Northern Ireland, occupies 5,459 square miles (14,139 square kilometers), or about 17 percent of the island. Northern Ireland is a partially self-governing province within the United Kingdom. This book focuses on the larger area—the Republic of Ireland, but because the two Irelands share many historical events and are located on the same island, there are many references to Northern Ireland.

One striking fact about the Emerald Isle and its two parts is their small size. The entire island of Ireland is approximately one fourth as large as Italy or Norway and about one twelfth the size of Egypt. Northern Ireland is only a little bigger than the state of Connecticut in the United States. The Republic of Ireland is not quite as large as the state of Maine.

The two Irelands may be small, but they have made many important contributions to the world. A number of great writers were born in Ireland. Among them are Jonathan Swift, George Bernard Shaw, William Butler Yeats, and James Joyce.

Many important events in the history of Christianity have occurred on the Emerald Isle. Saint Patrick, the most famous of the Irish saints and religious figures, introduced Christianity there during the fifth century A.D. The establishment of Christianity in Ireland contributed to the knowledge of all humans. During the period from about A.D. 476 to about 1000, often called the Dark Ages, learning and education declined in much of Europe. But Irish monks studying in monasteries were among the few who kept alive the knowledge gathered by past cultures. In this way Ireland's religious community helped to preserve Western civilization.

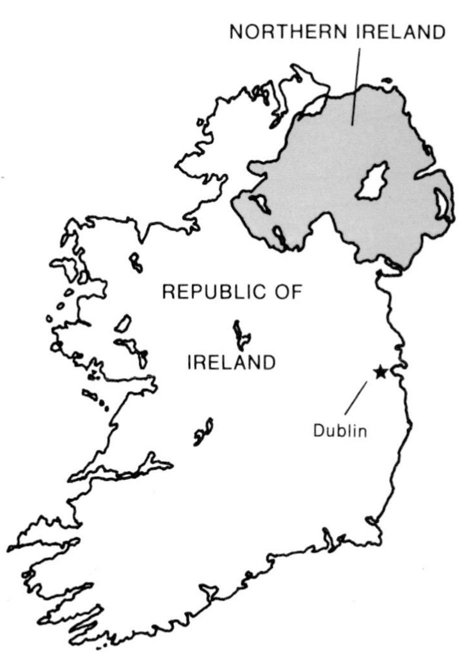

Cliffs of Moher, County Clare

Today, many aspects of Irish culture are popular outside the Emerald Isle. Saint Patrick's Day is celebrated in many countries by people who are not Irish and who have never seen Ireland. They dance the Irish jig and sing Irish folk songs. They eat Irish foods—including Irish stew and soda bread—and drink Irish whiskey and Irish stout. They tell stories about leprechauns, banshees, and other imaginary creatures from Irish folklore.

Unfortunately, this lovely island has had a history that has been filled with struggle and bloodshed. For more than seven hundred years, Ireland was ruled by England. Time and again the Irish people fought to free themselves. Not until 1921 did the Republic of Ireland gain independence from Britain. Northern Ireland is still part of the United Kingdom, which also includes England, Scotland, and Wales.

Killiney Bay, County Dublin

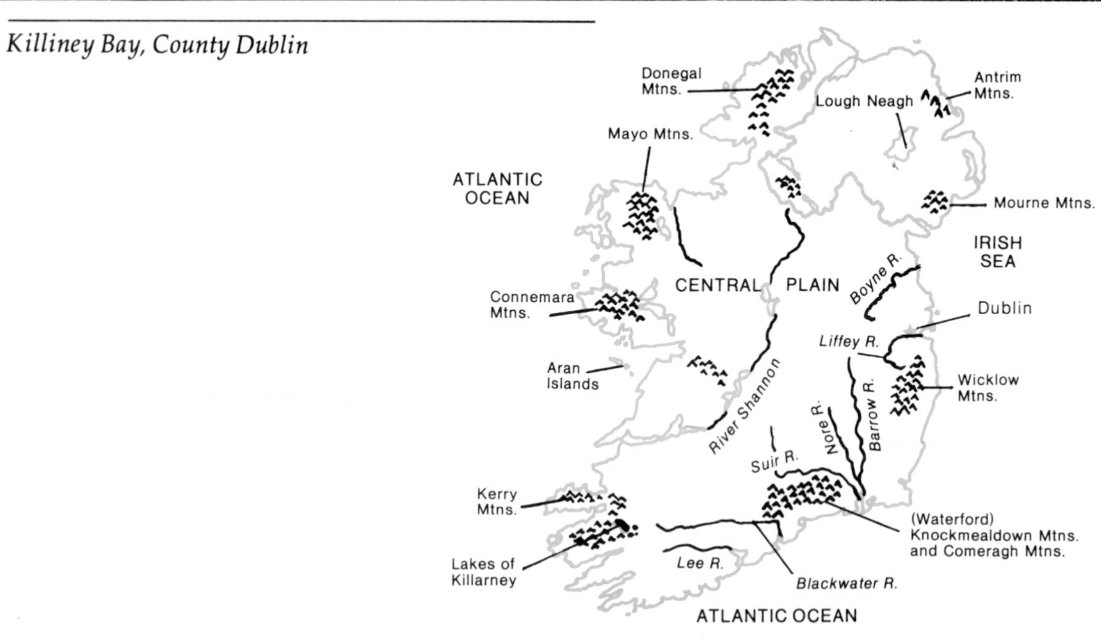

Chapter 2

THE LAND

In crisscrossing Ireland, it is the landscapes that stick in the mind, that come back in memory long after you have departed: Of the bleakness of Donegal, where thatched roofs of cottages are lashed down to hold against winter winds; and of the barrenness of Connemara and the Aran Islands, where crop soil is still fashioned from seaweed and sand, and the maze of field walls holds the countless stones handcleared from fields; of Galway Bay, the breaking up of a storm, the appearance of the sun, splintering the sky with colors.

John J. Putman, "A New Day for Ireland," in
April 1981 *National Geographic*

The people go, but the hills remain. Old Irish saying

GEOGRAPHY

The Republic of Ireland is in northwest Europe, bounded on the south, west, northwest, and part of the north by the Atlantic Ocean. To the east of most of the country is the Irish Sea, which separates the island from Great Britain. Northern Ireland, often inaccurately called Ulster, lies across a winding border in the northeast section of the island.

The Republic of Ireland has three principal types of land areas—seacoasts, mountain ranges, and a central plain. Because many

The Ring of Kerry (left) and cottages on Aran Island

ocean inlets, called bays, cut into the western and southern parts of the country, the republic has 1,738 miles (about 2,797 kilometers) of seacoast—a long coastal boundary for a small nation. There are dozens of small islands off the coast. These include Achill Island, Clare Island, Valentia Island, Dursey Island, and the famous Aran Islands.

A short way inland from the seacoasts stand numerous mountain ranges. In the west and southwest of the Irish coast the Mountains of Donegal, the Mountains of Mayo, the Mountains of Connemara, the Mountains of Kerry are major mountain ranges. The Republic of Ireland's highest point—Carrauntoohill—is in the Mountains of Kerry. Carrauntoohill's peak stands 3,414 feet (1041 meters) above sea level. The Wicklow Mountains are in the east.

Inland from the mountains is Ireland's heart—the central plain. Lovely green meadows and rich farmlands cover the central plain,

Lakes of Killarney on Ring of Kerry Drive (left) and the River Barrow, County Carlow

much of which has very fertile soil. Many crops are grown in this area, and extremely fine cattle and horses are raised here.

Thousands of years ago, during the Ice Ace, sheets of ice called glaciers covered Ireland. When the glaciers melted, the area that is now the Republic of Ireland was left with dozens of sparkling blue lakes. Among the most beautiful are the famous Lakes of Killarney in County Kerry.

The River Shannon is the longest and most famous river on the Emerald Isle. It begins in County Cavan in the north of the Republic of Ireland, winds for about 240 miles (386 kilometers), and empties into the Atlantic Ocean in the southwest. Other important rivers include the Boyne, the Moy, the Nore, the Suir, the Barrow, the Blackwater, the Lee, and the Liffey. The Republic of Ireland's largest city, Dublin, is located on the River Liffey, and Cork, the second largest, is on the Lee.

Glen da Lough Valley, County Wicklow

NATURAL RESOURCES

Of all the Irish Republic's natural treasures, fertile soil has always been one of the most important. Thanks to it, two thirds of the country is farmland. Of the country's many mineral treasures, zinc and lead are among the most valuable. Silver and copper are also mined.

Petroleum and natural gas are very important in today's world. The Republic of Ireland has long had to import these fuels—an expensive procedure. In recent years, gas and oil have been discovered beneath the sea in several places off the country's coast. The natural gas is already being utilized within the Republic of Ireland and the Irish hope that large-scale oil production will occur during the 1980s.

Peat is cut from bogs and used for both heating and cooking. You will see stacks of peat outside many Irish homes.

One substance long used as fuel in Ireland is peat, called turf by the Irish. Peat is composed of plants that have decayed in swamps and marshes. Peat bogs cover 15 percent of the Republic of Ireland. The peat is cut into bricks and dried and is then used in fireplaces to heat homes, in ovens as a cooking fuel, and to generate electricity in some power plants.

The country's large quantities of stone and rock, including limestone, granite, and marble, have been important for building. Since prehistoric times the Irish have used these materials to construct their dwellings, cathedrals, and other buildings.

Unfortunately, much of Ireland's wildlife has been killed off. The last wolves were killed in the late 1700s. All that remains of a giant deer, called the Irish elk, is its eight-foot-wide antlers, a number of which have been found in various places in the country. Today only a few kinds of animals—foxes, badgers, otters, red deer, and Irish hares—can be found in the wild. Among the sea life are herring, cod, lobsters, mackerel, and salmon.

Rural road in Westport, County Mayo. Croagh Patrick is in the background.

CLIMATE

The Republic of Ireland's climate is mild—summers rarely get very hot and winters rarely get very cold. Summer temperatures average around 60 degrees Fahrenheit (15.6 degrees Celsius). Winter temperatures average around 40 degrees Fahrenheit (4.4 degrees Celsius). Except in the mountains, snow is rare.

The Atlantic Ocean and the prevailing southwest wind combine to keep the climate mild. During the summer the ocean is cooler than the land. The wind carries that cooler air over Ireland, providing a free air-conditioning system. During the winter the ocean is warmer than the land, and its warm air provides a free heating system.

The ocean and the wind combine to present another gift to the island: plentiful rain. There is no season of the year and no part of the Republic of Ireland that is without rain for long. The

Fuschia hedges bloom in the peat-rich earth of County Galway.

mountains receive about 60 inches (152 centimeters) of rain per year. In the central plain the rainfall averages about 36 inches (about 91 centimeters) per year. Although rain may cause occasional floods, farmers usually welcome it. Abundant rainfall and fine soil result in fine crops.

The Irish weather can change rapidly. Any given day can contain morning mist, several rainstorms, and also periods of sparkling sunshine.

Because of that rapidly changing weather, the Irish countryside is a kaleidoscopic wonderland of color that photographers, artists, and writers have long tried to capture. When the air is filled with mist, everything is cloaked in greenish gray. When clouds cover the sun, the countryside is muted in various shades of gray and purple. When the sun peeks out from behind the clouds, the meadows and farmlands glow in gold and—of course!—countless shades of green.

Chapter 3

IN THE BEGINNING

I believe my countrymen (the English) will arrive. . . at the consciousness that the one deep and terrible stain upon their history, a history in most respects so noble, is to be found in their treatment of Ireland.

William E. Gladstone, nineteenth-century prime minister of Great Britain

They (the Irish) did battle often and valiantly against the stranger (the English). For centuries there was no day whereon someone did not lay a lance for Ireland; and Irish blood has reddened every inch of our soil.

P.S. O'Hegarty, *The Indestructible Nation*

PREHISTORIC PEOPLE

Ireland was one of the last European regions to be inhabited by human beings. Twenty thousand years ago, when early humans were already living in caves in France and Spain, the island of Ireland was still largely covered by ice sheets from the great Ice Age.

The oldest known evidence of people in Ireland dates from about ten thousand years ago, when the Ice Age ended. The island's first inhabitants are thought to have come by boat from southwestern Scotland. They settled along the coast of the Irish Sea in the northern and eastern parts of the island.

These first Irish people lived in the period of human history known as the Stone Age. They made their weapons out of stone, principally flint, which is found in great abundance in what is now Northern Ireland. Many of the leaf-shaped stone knives of the early Irish have been found near the Bann River in Northern Ireland, and so they are known as "Bann flakes."

The earliest Irish moved from place to place as they fished and hunted. By about six thousand years ago the Stone Age Irish were learning to grow crops and raise livestock. Farming brought a change in life-style, for it meant that people could settle down in one place. The farmers moved inland and began to build villages throughout the island.

Pottery, stone tools and weapons, ornaments, a few wooden houses, and other remains of the Stone Age farmers have been found on the Emerald Isle. A wooden house dating back 5,200 years was unearthed during the late 1960s near Cookstown in Northern Ireland. Wooden dwellings of Stone Age farmers have also been found in County Limerick and County Mayo in the Republic of Ireland.

Among the most interesting relics left by the Stone Age farmers are the tombs they built for their dead. Early people throughout the world often placed stones over graves to mark them. In Ireland many hundreds of Stone Age burial places have been found, including about three hundred so-called passage graves. Usually located on hilltops, passage graves are round dirt mounds with stone-covered burial chambers inside. A passage or tunnel leads from the entrance of the mound to the burial chamber. Passage graves on three hills—Dowth, Knowth, and Newgrange

This restoration of the Crannog and ring fort near Kilmurray was built on an artificial island in a lake. Furnished with replicas of implements, utensils, and other artifacts from the late Bronze Age, it reveals what life was like in 500 B.C.

in County Meath in the Republic of Ireland—comprise one of the most impressive Stone Age monuments ever found in western Europe.

The period following the Stone Age is known as the Bronze Age. During this era, people used the hard metal alloy bronze for their tools and weapons. In Ireland the Bronze Age began about four thousand years ago. The sturdy bronze weapons and tools made by the metalworking people enabled them to defend themselves better and to improve their ways of farming and styles of living. Daggers, axes, swords, and other bronze implements—as well as gold ornaments made by the Bronze Age people—can be seen in Irish museums today.

Bronze Age "hill forts," including Navan Fort near Armagh in Northern Ireland, have also been unearthed. The forts were constructed on hilltops and were surrounded by ditches. Some of the forts were used to protect the people, but others are thought to have been centers of religious worship.

THE CELTS

The Celts were an ancient people who dominated western and central Europe from about 500 B.C. to 1 B.C. About 400 B.C. Celtic tribes came to Ireland by boat from the European mainland and from the nearby island of Great Britain. The coming of the Celts marked the beginning of the Iron Age in Ireland. Brandishing their superior iron weapons, the Celts conquered the original Irish people and extended their rule over the entire island.

The Celts divided Ireland into a group of kingdoms, each of which was called a *tuath*. Each *tuath* was ruled by a Celtic chieftain, or king, called a *rí*. Sometimes several *tuatha* were combined into what was called a *mór-tuath*, ruled by an even more important king.

Starting in the third century A.D., much of Ireland was united under a single Celtic *Árd Rí*, or high king. The high king built a palace at the hill of Tara, overlooking the River Boyne. Tara served as the capital of Ireland. Here the high king made laws, arbitrated legal disputes, held games, and oversaw contests of music and verse making. One important high king was Niall of the Nine Hostages, who ruled from A.D. 380 to 405. He was reputed to have built five roads, all of which led to Tara. Today all that remains of the Celtic capital at Tara are a few ditches and some bumps in the ground where the buildings once stood.

Many aspects of Celtic culture, including laws, spread throughout Ireland. The Celtic kings had legal advisers, called *brehons*, who helped the kings make legal decisions regarding disputes. The laws, passed orally by the kings and *brehons* from generation to generation, became known as the Brehon Laws. Part of the purpose of the Brehon Laws was to protect the poor from those who were rich and powerful. The Brehon Laws were in effect for many centuries until the 1500s.

The Celts also brought their language, called Gaelic, to Ireland. A form of Gaelic, Irish Gaelic, often called Irish, is spoken in Ireland to this day. However, except for a form of lettering called *ogham* that was used on tombstones, the Celts had no written language. Their history and legends were told by poets and storytellers.

Many of the Celtic stories describe incredibly bloody wars fought between various kingdoms. The hero Cuchulainn is an important figure in the early stories. He was noted for his great size and beauty and for his skill and bravery. Of great help must have been the seven fingers on each hand, the seven toes on each foot, and seven pupils in each eye that the legends say he had. Cuchulainn was supposed to have defended the northern part of the island single-handedly against an entire army from the south.

Later stories tell of the hero Finn MacCool. Finn led a warrior band called the Fianna. To become a member, a young man had to be able to leap over branches as high as his forehead, run under branches at the level of his knees, and pick a thorn out of his foot while running at full speed. He also had to know numerous poems and old stories by heart.

So highly did the Celts regard storytelling that among their deities was Ogma, the god of eloquence and storytelling. Ogma was pictured as an old, bald man who drew crowds after him by golden chains attached to his tongue. The development of great Irish literature centuries later was due in part to the Celts' love of storytelling and poetry.

The Celts were polytheists—that is, they worshiped many gods. Celtic priests, called Druids, were believed to be able to tell the

The warrior Finn MacCool (left) and the hero Cuchulainn are important Celtic folk heroes.

future by studying the flights of birds and the insides of sacrificed animals. The Druids were sworn to secrecy, which is one reason why few details are known about their religion.

One interesting relic of the Celtic religion is Halloween. It began as a festival that honored Samhain, the god of death, whom the Celts associated with the coming of the cold season. The festival was later adapted by Roman and then Christian cultures, and it finally emerged as the day of witches, ghosts, and goblins that we know today.

SAINT PATRICK AND THE IMPACT OF CHRISTIANITY

Because the Celts lacked a system of writing, few concrete facts are known about Irish history before the fifth century. It is difficult to separate fact from legend concerning that early period. The 400s brought great changes. Christianity was brought to Ireland in that century. With Christianity came a new outlook on life, as well as a written language.

Celtic crosses (left) and St. Patrick, the patron saint of Ireland, are lasting reminders of the Irish dedication to Christianity.

Saint Patrick was the person most responsible for introducing Christianity to the Irish. Patrick was born somewhere on the island of Great Britain about the year 390. The exact place and date of his birth are not known. About 405, a raiding party sent out by Niall of the Nine Hostages captured a group of people in England, among them a young Christian boy named Patrick. Patrick was brought to the northern part of Ireland and made to work as a slave. During his years of tending pigs and sheep in Ireland, Patrick became very religious. After six years of slavery, he escaped and made his way home. He hoped, however, to return to Ireland one day to teach the people about Christianity.

Patrick studied to become a priest in France. Then, about 432, Pope Celestine I sent Patrick to Ireland. He went among the Irish people, asking them to give up their worship of many gods and telling them about Jesus Christ and Christianity.

As Patrick journeyed through the countryside, he also taught

Ruins on The Rock of Cashel (left) and an artist's view of a medieval monastery

people to read so that they could study the Bible on their own. Patrick is thought to have founded three hundred churches in Ireland and to have baptized more than 100,000 Irish persons.

Patrick is the patron saint of Ireland. The day of his death—March 17—is a national holiday in the Republic of Ireland. It is called Saint Patrick's Day.

The Irish countryside has many reminders of Saint Patrick. Croagh Patrick in County Mayo is a mountain where Patrick spent the forty days of Lent in the year 441. The Rock of Cashel in County Tipperary is where Patrick baptized a Munster king in 450. Lough Derg in County Donegal is a lake that Patrick visited.

The priests and saints of the 400s and the next several centuries had tremendous influence. Most of the Irish people gave up their worship of many gods and became Christians.

Christianity brought with it a climate of learning. Monasteries were built in many places throughout Ireland. Here religious men called monks lived and worked. The monks knew how to write in Latin and also developed a written language for Gaelic. The printing press had not yet been invented. Day after day the monks worked away, copying manuscripts by hand. The books they

Two pages from the Book of Kells written more than eleven hundred years ago

created were decorated with lovely designs and lettering. Since they seemed almost to glow with bright colors, they were called illuminated manuscripts.

One illuminated manuscript, the Book of Kells, included portions of the New Testament and some historical data. Completed in a monastery in the market town of Kells sometime in the 700s or 800s, the Book of Kells is often called the most beautiful book ever created. Deemed "the most purely Irish thing we have" by the twentieth-century Irish writer James Joyce, the Book of Kells is kept in the Trinity College Library in Dublin.

When the monks began to write in Gaelic, they recorded the early myths of Ireland. This is how we know about such legendary heroes as Cuchulainn and Finn MacCool.

The monks also studied science and mathematics. As early as the year 750 a man named Feargal proclaimed the earth to be round, not flat as most people then believed. About the year 800 a man named Ducuil made a geographical study of the known world.

Throughout most of Europe, civilization was at a low ebb during the Dark Ages. The knowledge gathered over centuries by the Greeks and Romans was forgotten as fierce tribes overran the continent. However, Ireland during those years enjoyed what is sometimes called its Golden Age, because the monks and scholars kept the light of knowledge alive. The Ireland of those years is sometimes referred to as the Island of Saints and Scholars.

It must be remembered, though, that the monks and scholars made up only a small number of people. The majority of the Irish were concerned primarily with raising enough livestock and growing enough crops to survive.

THE VIKING INVASIONS

The Vikings were the people of what are now Norway, Denmark, and Sweden. They were among the fiercest warriors who ever lived. They also built some of the sleekest and fastest ships of the time.

Starting about the year 795, Viking raiders left their overcrowded homelands and invaded Ireland. The Vikings sailed along the coasts and up the rivers of the island. They killed people, stole cattle, and destroyed property. They plundered monasteries, which contained valuable religious relics.

At first the Vikings returned home after their raids. Then some settled in Ireland. They built forts, which grew into Ireland's first cities. The cities of Dublin, Limerick, Cork, Waterford, Wexford, and Wicklow were all founded by the Vikings.

Viking power in Ireland reached its height about the year 1000,

Brian Boru, high king of Ireland

when the Vikings controlled a large portion of the island. Because the Irish had a number of different kings in various regions at this time, they lacked the unity needed to defeat the Vikings. Then in the year 1002, Brian Boru, a Christian, became high king of Ireland.

Brian Boru rebuilt the monasteries and churches that the Vikings had destroyed. He also built forts. In 1014, when Brian Boru was about seventy-four years old, he formed an army of thousands of Irishmen.

On Good Friday of 1014, Brian Boru's army met the Viking soldiers at Clontarf on the edge of Dublin. A fierce battle was fought, lasting from sunrise to sunset. Seven thousand Vikings were slain in what came to be known as the Battle of Brian or the Battle of Clontarf. Although four thousand Irish soldiers died in battle and Brian Boru was killed in his tent, King Brian's army was victorious. Because he ended the Vikings' hope of capturing all of Ireland, Brian Boru is remembered as one of Ireland's greatest heroes.

After their defeat, some of the Vikings sailed home. But many others stayed in Ireland and became Christians. As the Vikings, the Celts, and the original Irish intermarried, distinctions between the three groups disappeared. Their offspring all became part of the people called the Irish.

Norman tower at Johnstown Castle, County Wexford (left) and portrait of Henry II, the Norman king of England who invaded Ireland in 1171

ENGLISH RULE

For 150 years after Brian Boru's victory, Ireland was left undisturbed by outsiders. However, events were occurring in England that would soon affect Ireland. In 1066 the Normans (Vikings who settled in France) conquered England. Beginning in the late 1160s, Norman invaders from the island of Great Britain attacked Ireland. In 1169 the Norman earl of Pembroke, known as Strongbow, arrived in Ireland and soon made himself king of Leinster. Other Norman noblemen also took control of Irish lands. The Irish fought, but their soldiers, wearing simple tunics and equipped with swords and spears, had little chance against the Norman soldiers, who wore armor, rode swift horses, and had excellent weapons such as crossbows, longbows, giant catapults, and battering rams.

In 1171 Henry II, the Norman king of England, journeyed to Ireland with thousands of soldiers and knights. To make sure that the Irish people and the Normans who had seized land recognized his authority, Henry II declared himself king of Ireland. According to some historians, King Henry II had been encouraged by Pope

Adrian IV, the only Englishman ever to be pope, to claim Ireland for England. Henry's conquest began what was to be seven centuries of English rule.

The Normans gained more and more land until, by the 1300s, they controlled almost all of the Emerald Isle. The Norman nobles at first built wooden castles, and then later, stone castles. One of the most imposing castles still to be seen in Ireland is Trim Castle in County Meath. It was built about 1200. A poem of the time describes the building of Trim Castle:

> Then Hugh de Lacy
> Fortified a house at Trim
> And threw a fosse [trench] around it
> And then enclosed it with a herisson [stockade].
> Within the house he then placed
> Brave knights of great worth.

Other very old castles that can still be seen in what is now the Republic of Ireland include Limerick Castle (built about 1200) in the city of Limerick; Kilkenny and Granagh castles (both built in the thirteenth century) in County Kilkenny; Mallow Castle (built about 1282) in County Cork; and Roscommon and Ballintober castles (both built about 1300) in County Roscommon. In what is now Northern Ireland, Carrickfergus Castle (about 1180) can be seen at Belfast Lough; and Dundrum and Green castles (built about 1200 and 1261, respectively) can be seen along the Irish Sea in the southeastern part of the country.

For a while during the 1400s, the influence of the English (formerly the Normans) diminished in Ireland. One reason was that the English were busy fighting wars elsewhere. Another reason was that English people on the Emerald Isle married with

King Henry VIII

Queen Mary I

Queen Elizabeth I

the Irish and took on their language and way of life. It was even said that the English became "more Irish than the Irish themselves." In the early 1400s English influence in Ireland was restricted to a section in and around Dublin called The Pale.

In 1534, however, King Henry VIII of England renewed his country's interest in ruling Ireland. He had himself declared king of Ireland in 1541. The English then embarked on a massive program to deprive the Irish of their freedom and their very way of life.

Henry VIII's daughter, Mary I, became queen of England in 1553. Mary I began the colonization method known as "plantation." Rebel Irish families—at first in central Ireland—were evicted from their lands. English settlers or loyal Irish were then "planted" on those lands. Often the native Irish had to work for the English landlords or move to less desirable places.

Mary's sister, Elizabeth I, became queen of England in 1558. Called "Good Queen Bess" by her English subjects, Elizabeth I was hated by the Irish. One tremendous conflict that had developed between the Irish and the English concerned religion. The Irish were Catholics, while the English had turned to

Protestantism during the 1500s. The English tried to force the Irish to become Protestants, too. Despite intense persecution of all kinds, the Irish clung to their own religion. Elizabeth I ordered Irish-Catholic priests and bishops killed and outlawed Catholic religious services. She also seized 200,000 acres of Catholic-owned land and gave it to her fellow Englishmen.

Furious at what the English were doing to them, the Irish revolted again and again. During Elizabeth's time, the only part of the island the English didn't dominate was the north, where the O'Neill family was most prominent. In 1593 the O'Neills defeated the English in battle, and led other revolts soon after that. In 1601 Hugh O'Neill assembled an army of Irishmen and Spaniards, but was badly defeated by the English.

The next English ruler after Elizabeth I was James I, who was as cruel to the Irish as she had been. During the early 1600s James I cleared many of the Irish Catholics from the northern part of the island. In their place, he "planted" Scottish and English Protestants. This was a crucial event in the history of Ireland. The preponderance of Protestants in the northern part of the island and Catholics in the southern part created a situation resulting in conflicts that continue to this day.

Oliver Cromwell, who governed England from 1649 to 1658, continued the persecution of the Irish. An Irish revolt that had begun in 1641 was put down in 1649, when Cromwell invaded Ireland with a huge army. Among the slaughters perpetrated by the English at this time was Cromwell's ruthless killing of more than 3,500 men, women, and children at Drogheda on the eastern coast of Ireland. After overcoming the Irish, Cromwell gave more of their lands to his soldiers. So many Irish were either killed or fled the island between 1641 and 1650 that in those few years

James I (far left) and James II (left)

Ireland's population dropped from an estimated 1.5 million to less than 1 million. Those who remained had to live on desolate lands, most of which were on the west coast of Ireland in Connacht Province.

The expression "Hell or Connacht" was often uttered in despair by the Irish during this time. Other than Connacht Province, the Irish had little choice of where to go.

The English completely dominated the Emerald Isle. By the middle 1650s, four-fifths of Ireland had been taken over by English landlords. By the late 1600s, the English had seized more than 85 percent of Irish lands.

The Irish people had hope again in 1685 when James II, a Catholic, became England's king. He temporarily ended persecution of the Catholic Irish. However, James II had his own problems. The crown was taken from him and given to his Protestant daughter, Mary II, and her husband, William III.

In an effort to regain his crown, James II, with French support, went to Ireland, where he had numerous followers. He formed an army of Irish Catholics, which was supplemented by many French officers. Meanwhile, Protestants from the northern part of Ireland augmented William's army of Dutch and Englishmen. The two armies met in 1690, on the banks of the River Boyne. William won the Battle of the Boyne. After this—if it can be imagined—conditions were worse than ever for the Irish Catholics.

During the 1700s the Catholics were treated much as black slaves were treated in America. The English passed a series of cruel Penal Laws. These laws established severe fines and imprisonment for taking part in Catholic worship. They also forced more of the Irish to give up their lands. By the late 1770s the Irish Catholics, who then made up 75 percent of the population in Ireland, owned just 5 percent of the land. The Irish had to work for English or Anglo-Irish Protestant landlords on property that once had been their own.

Because the English had placed a heavy tax on homes with fireplaces, many of the Irish lived in unheated shacks. In addition, they had little to eat but potatoes. Their chilly homes and lack of nourishing food made the Irish subject to illness.

According to the Penal Laws, no Irish Catholic was allowed to vote, buy property, hold public office, own a gun, or own a horse worth more than five pounds. Catholics were barred from becoming lawyers or teachers. Because Catholic worship was forbidden, the Irish had to hold secret services out in the fields. Catholic schools also were illegal. Some Irish children attended Protestant schools. Others went to "hedge schools," which were secret schools often held outdoors in secluded places. Some Irish children didn't go to school at all.

The Irish fought English oppression in two ways. The first was to attempt to change things through the law. The other way to change things was by armed conflict.

In 1798 Theobald Wolfe Tone (far left) and in 1803 Robert Emmet (left) led rebellions against English rule. Both revolutions failed.

TWO REVOLUTIONARIES: THEOBALD WOLFE TONE AND ROBERT EMMET

England in the late 1700s and early 1800s was one of the most powerful nations on earth. The Irish had virtually no chance to defeat the mighty English army; yet there were a number of Irish patriots who were willing to risk their lives in pursuit of liberty.

Theobald Wolfe Tone (1763-1798), a Dublin lawyer, was one of those who decided to fight. In 1791 Tone helped found the Society of United Irishmen in Belfast. The Society's goal was to form a united Ireland, free of England.

In January of 1796 Tone went to France, which was then at war with England. The French promised to help the Irish in their rebellion. In December of that year fifteen thousand French soldiers sailed with Tone for Bantry Bay in County Cork, but bad weather forced them to turn around and return home.

In 1798 the United Irishmen rose up against the English in many areas of Ireland and were promptly beaten. Tone and other leaders of the United Irishmen were captured. Denied a soldier's firing squad execution and condemned to be hanged as a traitor, Theobald Wolfe Tone committed suicide in prison in November of 1798. Others were executed.

Of all the rebellions, one of the most hopeless was led by a young man named Robert Emmet. His revolt became a symbol of the Irish spirit of rebellion against overwhelming odds.

Born in Dublin in 1778, Robert Emmet was the last of seventeen children. Only Robert and three others survived childhood, although Robert's father was a doctor and the Emmet family was well-to-do. The death rate was often worse among poor Irish families, who lived in cramped, unhealthy conditions.

Although the Emmets were Protestants, they, like many other Protestants in Ireland, were angered by the plight of the Catholics. At the dinner table, Robert often heard his father speak of Irish independence. At the age of twelve, Robert Emmet wrote a poem that began: "Brothers, arise, our country calls. Let us gain her rights or die."

Young Robert Emmet didn't fight in Theobald Wolfe Tone's rebellion of 1798. But that year he was expelled from Dublin's Trinity College because of his patriotic talk and because he belonged to the Society of United Irishmen.

Shortly after 1800, Robert Emmet decided it was time for Ireland to "gain her rights or die." He spoke to people who had fought in the rebellion of 1798 and told them of his bold plan. He and some followers would seize Dublin Castle, the center of English government in Ireland. Once the castle was secure, fires would be lighted and rockets launched to signal the people of Dublin and throughout Ireland to revolt.

Emmet and his men turned five buildings in Dublin into

arsenals, where they stored weapons and ammunition. Robert also rented a house on Butterfield Lane as a hideout.

The date was set for the revolt—Saturday, July 23, 1803. On that day, Emmet and several dozen others met in their Dirty Lane headquarters. Robert gathered up hundreds of the proclamations he had had printed, planning to distribute them to the Dubliners. "OUR OBJECT IS TO ESTABLISH A FREE AND INDEPENDENT REPUBLIC IN IRELAND," these handbills stated. Emmet then put on his green and gold uniform and prepared to lead his men against the English soldiers.

Everything went wrong. Someone had spread the rumor that the battle had been postponed. Because of this, many of Emmet's best men were unprepared. Then there was a second disaster. To avoid being seen, Emmet and his men had planned to go to Dublin Castle in coaches rather than on foot. But the man in charge of delivering the coaches was stopped by a suspicious army officer and never reached headquarters. Robert and his men were left to walk to the castle with their weapons in plain sight.

By now Robert Emmet and his men figured that the English knew of their plans. Some wanted to run away. Realizing that the English would hunt them down anyway, Emmet said, "We might as well die fighting—come on, my boys!" He then led his men out of the Dirty Lane arsenal. As they passed Dubliners on the street, Emmet said, "Turn out, my boys, now is your time for liberty. Liberty, my boys!"

Largely because of the rumor that the battle had been postponed, Emmet had only eighty men instead of the two thousand he had expected. They never reached Dublin Castle. Emmet's small army was joined by a mob from the Dublin taverns. These people, many of them drunk on that Saturday night, stopped a coach and killed two innocent people—the

English Lord Kilwarden and his nephew. Seeing that his revolt had led to senseless murder, Emmet told his men to scatter.

On his way to the Butterfield Lane hideout, Emmet was stopped by a policeman. The policeman fired shots, but Emmet managed to wound him with his sword and escape.

Robert Emmet and his lieutenants spent the night at the hideout and then moved on. As Emmet moved about the countryside, English soldiers were always in pursuit. On August 25, 1803, soldiers burst into the house where he was hiding. Emmet was arrested and jailed.

There was no doubt that Robert Emmet would be sentenced to death. Yet this was really just the beginning of his story. As a revolutionary, he had been a failure. He had counted too much on other people, had poor organization, and had men who were not trained for battle. All this was understandable. Emmet was a thinker and a speaker, not a fighter.

Once in court, Robert Emmet put his true abilities to work. The trial took one long day—from 9:30 in the morning until 10:30 at night on September 19, 1803. Each time a witness spoke against him, Emmet told his lawyers, "Don't try to defend me—it's no use." Finally the time came when Robert Emmet could speak before being sentenced. His words became so famous that Irish children were repeating them 150 years later.

"My lords," he began, "as to why judgment of death and execution should not be passed on me according to law, I have nothing to say." Emmet explained that he had wanted "to make Ireland totally independent of Great Britain," and predicted that the Irish would revolt again and again until they were free.

Although sorry about the deaths that had occurred, Emmet called them a result of English oppression. "My ministry is now ended," Emmet continued. "I am going to my cold and silent grave—my lamp of life is nearly extinguished. I have parted with everything that was dear to me in this life for my country's cause. . . . "

Then came words that brought tears to the eyes of many in the courtroom, including the English judge. "Let no man write my epitaph!" Emmet said, in a clear, ringing voice. "When my country takes her place among the nations of the earth, then, and not till then, let my epitaph be written. I have done."

Robert Emmet was hanged the next day. As a grisly reminder that England would utterly destroy all rebels, Robert Emmet's body was beheaded. He was buried in an unmarked grave. Those who knew its location kept silent.

Where Robert Emmet's body was buried wasn't important. His name, deeds, and words were forever engraved in the hearts of the Irish. Paintings of Emmet were hung on cottage walls throughout Ireland. Thousands of songs and poems were composed about "The Darlin' of Erin," as he was called. Children memorized Emmet's speech and recited it word for word at family gatherings. Even Abraham Lincoln, in a cabin in faraway Kentucky, learned the speech. To people everywhere, Robert Emmet came to symbolize Ireland's quest for independence.

WORKING WITHIN THE LAW

Despite the drama of Tone's and Emmet's revolts, during the late 1700s and the 1800s the Irish made more headway by working through the law than by using bullets. It must be added, though, that these doomed rebellions made the English aware that they had to improve conditions in Ireland.

Daniel O'Connell, the "liberator" of Ireland, (left). The Catholic Association formed by O'Connell gained the support of the Irish peasants. It was the beginning of modern Irish nationalism and the model for all organizations that fought for reform in nineteenth century Ireland and Britain.

After Tone's rebellion of 1798, the English made Ireland part of Great Britain. The law that accomplished this, the Act of Union of 1801, made Ireland part of what was called the United Kingdom of Great Britain and Ireland. The Irish were then allowed to send representatives to Parliament, England's lawmaking body. But only Protestants could be sent to Parliament from Ireland, and only those Catholics who paid a certain amount of rent to the Protestant landlords were even allowed to vote.

Daniel O'Connell, born in County Kerry, worked in the early 1800s for the rights of Catholics. As a boy O'Connell had gone to a hedge school. Later, as a lawyer, he saved so many poor Irish people from being deported or executed that he was nicknamed the "King of the Beggars." In 1823 O'Connell formed the Catholic Association to work for the rights of Ireland's Catholics. Then in 1828 O'Connell won an election to represent Country Clare, Ireland, in the English Parliament but was not allowed to take his seat because he was a Catholic. The English realized, however, that continuing to deny O'Connell the seat he had won by election would generate more Irish protest. In 1829 England passed the Catholic Emancipation Act, which allowed Catholics to be admitted to the English Parliament. Because of his work in gaining rights for Ireland's Catholics through legal means,

O'Connell is remembered as the "Liberator," and is considered one of the greatest of all Irish patriots.

THE POTATO FAMINE

For the millions of Irish who were landless, powerless, and hungry, the right to take part in the English Parliament meant little. Their main problem was surviving from year to year, or even from day to day. In 1835 the Frenchman Alexis de Tocqueville wrote about the pathetic way of life of the Irish: "Mud walls; thatched roofs; one room; no chimney; smoke comes out of the door. . . the population looks very wretched. Most of them are dressed in clothes with holes or very much patched. Most of them are barefoot and bare-headed."

Hunger became Ireland's major problem in the 1840s. At that time, more than half of the eight million people in Ireland lived in little huts and ate little or nothing besides potatoes. From 1845 to 1847 much of Ireland's potato crop was destroyed by a disease. Millions of people had absolutely *nothing* to eat. A man named Cummins of Cork described the famine in the town of Skibbereen, but his words could have been written about much of Ireland at that time:

> . . . six famished and ghastly skeletons, to all appearance dead, were huddled in a corner on some filthy straw, their sole covering what seemed a ragged horse-cloth, and their wretched legs hanging about, naked above the knees. I. . . found by a low moaning, they were alive. . . . The same morning the police opened a house on the adjoining lands. . . and two frozen corpses were found lying upon the mud floor.

Seventy-two-year-old Daniel O'Connell warned the British Parliament that "Ireland is in your hands. . . one-quarter of her population will perish unless you come to her relief." England did respond, but not enough food or help was sent in time. A million died of starvation or disease in Ireland because of the Potato Famine, or the "Great Hunger," as it was called. Yet even while the famine raged through the land, food crops and cattle were sold and shipped to England.

During the famine more than a million Irish people boarded ships and sailed for the United States and other lands. Mr. and Mrs. S.C. Hall described the departure of the Irish during the famine years:

> We stood in the month of June on the quay at Cork to see some emigrants embark in one of the steamers for Falmouth, on the way to Australia. The band of exiles amounted to two hundred, and an immense crowd had gathered to bid them a long and last adieu. The scene was touching to a degree; it was impossible to witness it without heart-pain and tears. Mothers hung upon the necks of their athletic sons; young girls clung to elder sisters; fathers—old white-haired men—fell to their knees, with arms uplifted to heaven, imploring the protecting care of the Almighty on their departing children. . . .
>
> Amid the din, the noise, the turmoil, the people pressing and rolling in vast masses towards the place of embarkation like the waves of the troubled sea, there were many such sad episodes. Men, old men too, embracing each other and crying like children. Several passed

Traveling in cramped, crowded quarters, more than a million people fled Ireland during the Potato Famine. Many emigrated to the United States.

> bearing most carefully little relics of their homes—the branch of a favorite hawthorn tree, whose sweet blossoms and green leaves were already withered, or a bunch of meadowsweet.
>
> It is impossible to describe the final parting. Shrieks and prayers, blessings and lamentations mingled in one great cry from those on the quay, and those on shipboard, until a band stationed on the forecastle struck up "St. Patrick's Day."

Weakened by hunger and illness, thousands of Irish emigrants died on the overseas voyages. The population of Ireland, which had stood at 8 million before the famine, was reduced to 5.5 million by 1851. Largely because of the Potato Famine, even today Ireland's population is only about half of what it was in 1845.

MORE FIGHTS ON THE BATTLEFIELD AND IN THE LAW CHAMBERS

According to Irish leaders, English oppression, rather than a plant disease, was the real cause of the Potato Famine. They claimed it had occurred because the English and the Anglo-Irish landlords kept the Irish poor, hungry, and dependent on one crop. The survivors of the famine listened to these leaders.

In 1858 a new drive for Irish independence was begun in Ireland and Britain by the Irish Republican Brotherhood. In the United States, where many Irish people had settled, a secret society called the Fenian Brotherhood was formed. The Fenians—who took their name from Finn MacCool's legendary warrior band—believed in complete Irish independence. To accomplish their goal, the Fenians set off bombs and led several uprisings. In London, a blast they set off to release two Fenians from prison killed at least twelve people and injured many more. In Manchester, England, three American Fenians, trying to rescue one of their leaders, allegedly killed a policeman. The three Americans were hanged. In 1867 the Fenian revolt, like all the previous Irish revolts, was put down.

While the Fenians engaged in battle, others continued the legal fight. Home rule became an important issue in the 1870s and 1880s. Home rule would give the Irish self-government in matters within the Emerald Isle. Great Britain would maintain control over Ireland's relations with the rest of the world.

Charles Stewart Parnell became a champion of the home rule movement. In 1875 Parnell was elected to the British Parliament from County Meath, Ireland. Parnell became president of the Land League, an organization that worked to allow farmers to pay

Charles Stewart Parnell, the Protestant founder of the Irish Party, was perhaps Ireland's greatest statesman. He fought for Irish Catholic rights and Irish Home Rule in Britain's parliament and achieved reform through law.

lower rents to their landlords and eventually to own their own farms. William Gladstone, prime minister of Great Britain, also supported home rule for Ireland, as well as laws to aid Ireland's tenant farmers. Parnell and Gladstone were successful in achieving fairer treatment for tenant farmers, but English lawmakers defeated home rule bills in 1886 and again in 1892. One reason for the failure of the home rule bills was that Ireland's Protestants, who lived mainly in the northern part of the island, opposed home rule. They were afraid they would suffer if the Catholic majority began to govern the affairs of Ireland.

The growing nationalistic feeling of the Irish people was further inspired in 1893 when Douglas Hyde and Eoin MacNeill founded the Gaelic League. The league's goal was to revive the ancient Gaelic language and to make Gaelic stories, music, dancing, and history known to the Irish people. Soon Irish poets were writing in Gaelic and children in hundreds of schools were learning the language. The Gaelic League helped the Irish people recognize and

Padraic Henry Pearse led the 1916 Easter Rebellion against British rule. The revolt was designed to take advantage of Britain's involvement in World War I. Troops that might have been fighting in Europe had to be sent to Ireland to end the rebellion.

take pride in the fact that they had an ancient heritage separate from England's.

In the late 1890s Arthur Griffith, a Dublin printer, founded a newspaper called *The United Irishman.* In his newspaper Griffith wrote that, instead of sending lawmakers to the English Parliament, Ireland should set up its own government at home. In 1905 Griffith founded a society called Sinn Féin ("Ourselves Alone" in Gaelic). The Sinn Féin society urged the Irish to refuse to pay English-imposed taxes and to work for Irish independence. In the early 1900s supporters of Sinn Féin and thousands of others were again talking revolution.

THE EASTER REBELLION

At the beginning of the twentieth century the Irish Republican Brotherhood, which had spawned the Fenian revolt of 1867, was being revived. The Brotherhood was led by one of the most remarkable persons ever born in Ireland—Padraic Pearse. A poet and story writer, Pearse was headmaster of St. Enda's School in

The Irish rebels set up barricades in the streets to stop the advance of the heavily armed British troops.

Rathfarnham, where his students learned Gaelic and were taught about the heroes of old. Like Robert Emmet, Pearse was a thinker who was prepared to fight.

In early 1916 Pearse, along with other members of the Irish Republican Brotherhood, Sinn Féin members, and other revolutionaries, planned an armed revolt. Originally scheduled to take place in Dublin on Easter Sunday, at the last moment the rebellion was rescheduled for the next day.

On Monday, April 24, 1916, Padraic Pearse led his troops out of Liberty Hall in central Dublin. Pearse and his followers were aware of all the previous failed rebellions. They knew that they couldn't win. As James Connolly, one of the leaders, left Liberty Hall, he said to a friend, "We're going out to be slaughtered, you know."

The revolutionaries spread out and seized various buildings in Dublin. Pearse led the group that seized the post office and raised a green, white, and orange flag over the building. Then Pearse stood on the steps of the post office and read this proclamation:

POBLACHT NA H EIREANN.

THE PROVISIONAL GOVERNMENT
OF THE
IRISH REPUBLIC
TO THE PEOPLE OF IRELAND.

IRISHMEN AND IRISHWOMEN: In the name of God and of the dead generations from which she receives her old tradition of nationhood, Ireland, through us, summons her children to her flag and strikes for her freedom.

Having organised and trained her manhood through her secret revolutionary organisation, the Irish Republican Brotherhood, and through her open military organisations, the Irish Volunteers and the Irish Citizen Army, having patiently perfected her discipline, having resolutely waited for the right moment to reveal itself, she now seizes that moment, and, supported by her exiled children in America and by gallant allies in Europe, but relying in the first on her own strength, she strikes in full confidence of victory.

We declare the right of the people of Ireland to the ownership of Ireland, and to the unfettered control of Irish destinies, to be sovereign and indefeasible. The long usurpation of that right by a foreign people and government has not extinguished the right, nor can it ever be extinguished except by the destruction of the Irish people. In every generation the Irish people have asserted their right to national freedom and sovereignty; six times during the past three hundred years they have asserted it in arms. Standing on that fundamental right and again asserting it in arms in the face of the world, we hereby proclaim the Irish Republic as a Sovereign Independent State, and we pledge our lives and the lives of our comrades-in-arms to the cause of its freedom, of its welfare, and of its exaltation among the nations.

The Irish Republic is entitled to, and hereby claims, the allegiance of every Irishman and Irishwoman. The Republic guarantees religious and civil liberty, equal rights and equal opportunities to all its citizens, and declares its resolve to pursue the happiness and prosperity of the whole nation and of all its parts, cherishing all the children of the nation equally, and oblivious of the differences carefully fostered by an alien government, which have divided a minority from the majority in the past.

Until our arms have brought the opportune moment for the establishment of a permanent National Government, representative of the whole people of Ireland and elected by the suffrages of all her men and women, the Provisional Government, hereby constituted, will administer the civil and military affairs of the Republic in trust for the people.

We place the cause of the Irish Republic under the protection of the Most High God, Whose blessing we invoke upon our arms, and we pray that no one who serves that cause will dishonour it by cowardice, inhumanity, or rapine. In this supreme hour the Irish nation must, by its valour and discipline and by the readiness of its children to sacrifice themselves for the common good, prove itself worthy of the august destiny to which it is called.

Signed on Behalf of the Provisional Government,

THOMAS J. CLARKE,

SEAN Mac DIARMADA, THOMAS MacDONAGH,

P. H. PEARSE, EAMONN CEANNT,

JAMES CONNOLLY. JOSEPH PLUNKETT.

The seven men who signed this proclamation were executed for their part in the Easter Rebellion.

Ruins of Sackville Street in Dublin after the British troops had put down the rebellion.

It was a declaration of Ireland's independence. Pearse and his fellow revolutionaries had declared their country free of England—just as the United States had done 140 years earlier.

The revolutionaries had hoped that eventually ten thousand men and women would join their revolt. However, no more than fifteen hundred ever joined: Dubliners knew that taking part in the revolution would very likely mean death.

While Pearse and his men held the Dublin post office, the English amassed an army of twelve thousand soldiers. The streets of Dublin were filled with machine-gun, rifle, and even cannon fire during the week-long battle. The shelling set the whole center of Dublin ablaze. Finally the superior English forces put down the Easter Rebellion, called that because it was fought right after Easter. Fifty years later, Sean Nunan, who fought in the Easter Rebellion, described what had happened at the Dublin post office.

> Nobody believed what was happening as we ordered everyone out and took over [the post office]. I was ordered to build a barricade. Near the post office was a museum in which life-sized figures of famous men of the day were exhibited. I grabbed the effigies of King George V [then king of England] and Lord Kitchener

> and put them to work for Ireland. We had bombs, shotguns, rifles. The lucky ones had Lee-Enfield 303s. They got their first use as we opened fire on mounted British lancers riding up O'Connell Street to dislodge us. I remember James Connolly, wounded, calling to me from a stretcher to take a message to Padraic Pearse. . . . I found Pearse and told him.
>
> On Thursday the British gunboat *Helga* got the range on the post office from the Liffey. The building began to burn from top to bottom. We carried bombs and provisions out to safety. As we evacuated I was told to engage a sniper hitting us from the old Gresham Hotel. My brother joined me. We could do nothing. The enemy was too well covered.
>
> I recall Mick Collins at the barricades with a pistol. The body of The O'Rahilly [an Irish leader] lay dead in a doorway. Padraic Pearse was at the door with a word as we left. Sean McDermott [also known as Sean MacDiarmada] told us we were surrendering. "Come along, gentlemen," said the British officer who took the surrender. "I call you gentlemen because you made a brave fight of it."

The results of the Easter Rebellion were horrifying: 1,351 dead, 2,500 wounded, 179 buildings destroyed, and more than 3,500 men and 79 women arrested.

Fifteen Irish leaders were executed, including all seven who had signed the proclamation of independence. On the night before he was executed, Sean MacDiarmada wrote: "We die that the Irish nation may live. Our blood will rebaptise and reinvigorate the land." Just before his execution Padraic Pearse wrote to his mother: "This is the death I should have asked for, if God had given me the choice of all deaths. . . a soldier's death for Ireland and freedom." One rebel leader, James Connolly, was so badly wounded that the English had to carry him to the execution yard on a stretcher. They strapped him to a chair and shot him dead.

The imprisonments and brutal executions incensed the Irish as well as many people in England and the United States. In this way, the Easter Rebellion defeat—like the earlier ones—fueled the flame of Irish nationalism and the Irish continued to fight for liberty. In 1918 Sinn Féin Irish lawmakers elected to the British Parliament refused to go to London. These lawmakers set up their own government (called the *Dáil Éireann*—the House of Deputies) in Dublin, and on January 21, 1919 they reaffirmed the republic proclaimed by the leaders of the Easter Rebellion.

It took more bloodshed to make that declaration a reality. The Irish Republican Army (IRA) was formed in 1919 by people who wanted an independent Ireland. Led by "The Big Fellow" Michael Collins, the IRA raided English police barracks and ambushed patrols. In turn, the English formed an armed police force called the Black and Tans. There are elderly people in Ireland today who still remember how these two groups sprayed the streets with gunfire during the early 1920s.

England could see that eventually Ireland was going to make itself independent. However, English politicians also saw that there were two main groups of people on the island—the Catholics and the Protestants. The Catholics—who constituted roughly 75 percent of the population at that time—lived mainly in the southern five-sixths of the island. Most of the Catholics wanted Ireland to be a single, independent country, completely separate from England.

The Protestants—who were roughly 25 percent of the population—lived mainly in the northern one-sixth of the island. Many of these Protestants were descendants of the Protestants from England and Scotland who had been planted in northern Ireland in the 1600s. Most of the Protestants wanted Ireland—or at least the northern part of the island—to remain a part of the United Kingdom.

As a compromise in 1920 the British Parliament passed the Government of Ireland Act, which divided Ireland into two separate, self-governing parts, each of which would still be part of Great Britain. The larger country would be composed of twenty-six counties. The smaller one in the northeastern part of the island would be composed of six counties.

The six northeastern counties accepted this act and they officially became Northern Ireland. Great Britain was renamed the United Kingdom of Great Britain and Northern Ireland to acknowledge the fact that Northern Ireland remained in the kingdom, which already included England, Scotland, and Wales.

Lawmakers in the twenty-six southern counties rejected the Government of Ireland Act. They objected to the idea that an Ireland with Home Rule would still be under the ultimate authority of the British Parliament. Also, most people in the south still wanted a single, united Ireland.

Fighting between the English Black and Tans and the IRA continued. Finally, in July 1921, a truce was arranged between England and the Irish revolutionaries. For five months Irish lawmakers negotiated with the English. Then, at 2:30 on the morning of December 6, 1921, English and Irish officials signed a treaty. According to this treaty, the twenty-six counties comprising the southern five-sixths of Ireland would be a self-governing dominion of Great Britain; that is, the country would govern itself but would still acknowledge the English monarch as chief of state. This new country was called the Irish Free State.

Thus, dawn of December 6, 1921, found the island of Ireland partitioned with a border that remains to this day. In the northeast was Northern Ireland, which was part of the United Kingdom of Great Britain and Northern Ireland and still had close ties to England. In the south was the Irish Free State (later the Republic of Ireland), which still had some ties to England but was much more independent.

This political solution to the Irish question did not solve the problem. More troubles were coming. Many people in the Irish Free State were very bitter that their country had been sliced in two. They were prepared to fight as long as it took to create what Theobald Wolfe Tone, Robert Emmet, Padraic Pearse, and so many others had died trying to create: one Ireland totally free of England.

Chapter 4

AND THEN THERE WERE TWO

The Irish government does not concede in any way, and never will, Britain's right to exercise jurisdiction over any part of Irish territory. . . . The claim of the Irish nation to control the totality of Ireland has been asserted over the centuries by successive generations of Irishmen and women and it is one which will never be renounced.

John Lynch, prime minister of the Republic of Ireland, speaking in 1969

We have conditioned our people to think in terms of a long struggle. We don't speculate how long it will take. We did make the mistake early on of predicting armed victory in successive years. . . . We have suffered too much, and come through too much, to settle for anything less than full freedom. We have the determination, and resolve, and the resources, to keep going until we get the Brits [the English] out.

Anonymous Provisional IRA leader in a 1979 Dublin *Sunday Press* newspaper interview

After the formation of the Irish Free State in 1921, peace was still impossible on the Emerald Isle. Two main issues divided the people. First, there were many in the Irish Free State who despised their country's status as an English dominion and wanted to see it completely independent of England. As a dominion, the Irish Free State was forced to retain English naval bases. Also, the country's lawmakers had to take an oath of allegiance to the British king.

An even more troubling matter was the division of the island into two parts. Many of the Irish Free State's Catholic majority were bitter about this, as were many of Northern Ireland's Catholics, who made up one-third of that area's population. These northern Catholics felt that they had more in common with the Catholics to the south than with their Protestant fellow-citizens.

England clearly had created this divisiveness within the Emerald Isle by controlling Ireland for so many centuries and by planting the Protestants in the north during the 1600s. It is not so easy to determine a right and wrong side among the people who lived on the island.

Consider the case of the Catholics. It has already been chronicled that the Catholics lived on the island centuries before the Protestants and that they were moved off their own land and treated much like slaves. Certainly it is easy to see the Catholics' argument that—although obviously they couldn't get their northern lands back—at least the island should be reunited. There should be only one, united, independent country called Ireland.

The Protestants in Northern Ireland had a strong argument, too. Their ancestors had been moved to the north of the island in the early 1600s. This meant that, in 1921, the Protestants had lived there for just over three hundred years. The Protestants felt that those three centuries gave them the right to their own country, regardless of the unjust events of the past. And politically they wanted to retain their ties with England.

Eamon de Valera, in 1923

John A. Costello, in 1956

As in the previous history of Ireland, these differences of opinion were pursued in two ways—through legal channels and by force of arms.

Eamon de Valera, who had fought in the Easter Rebellion, was the leading spokesman for those who wanted one Ireland totally independent of England. This group constituted the antitreaty forces who opposed the 1921 treaty that partitioned Ireland. William Cosgrave, president of the executive council that governed the Irish Free State, spoke for those who supported the 1921 treaty—the protreaty forces.

The IRA wanted Ireland to be an independent republic, not a dominion within the British Commonwealth. In 1922 and 1923 the IRA and others fought with those who supported the treaty. The fighting during this period is known as the Irish Civil War.

It is important to remember that the Irish Civil War did not involve Northern Ireland's fighting the Irish Free State. It involved protreaty people fighting antitreaty people within each section. There were shootings, assassinations, and executions on both sides. Finally, the IRA and other antitreaty forces were defeated in May of 1923. There had been at least five hundred deaths in the Irish Civil War. Although the antitreaty forces had lost, they weren't ready to stop fighting.

In 1932 Eamon de Valera became president of the Executive Committee of the Irish Free State, serving in that position until 1937. Working within the law to free his country from England, de Valera cut ties with England while he was head of the government and did away with the oath of allegiance to the king that lawmakers in the Irish Free State despised. A new constitution in 1937 broke more ties with England, and in 1938 England abandoned its right to maintain naval bases in the Irish Free State. As prime minister de Valera negotiated the new agreement with the British government.

The leaders of the Irish Free State severed more and more ties with England until, in late 1948, Prime Minister John A. Costello of the Irish Free State introduced a bill to the country's lawmakers that "will end, and end forever, in a simple unequivocal way, the country's long and tragic association with the British Crown." The bill passed unanimously and on April 18, 1949 the government of the Irish Free State declared Ireland a totally independent republic. They named the new state the Republic of Ireland—the name by which it is known today. Thus, after seven centuries of battle, the Republic of Ireland, comprising five-sixths of the island, stood separate from England. This still left the northeastern corner of the island—Northern Ireland—as part of Great Britain.

Most people in any country are more interested in making a living and in decent living conditions than in politics. In the 1950s and 1960s the Catholics in Northern Ireland became increasingly vocal about various kinds of social and economic discrimination that oppressed them in their daily lives. For one thing, it was difficult for the Catholic minority to achieve positions in government or in good-paying professions. The Catholics often lived in poor neighborhoods and their lack of education and training led to high unemployment. In the 1960s Northern

Two members of the illegal Ulster Volunteer Force at machine gun practice (far left). Armed members of the rebel IRA, called Provisionals, patrol the upper Falls area of Belfast in a stolen land rover (middle). Rioters stone a fallen British soldier during a violent demonstration (right).

Ireland's Catholics formed civil rights groups to end this social and economic discrimination. They also demonstrated and held marches. In retaliation, Protestants held their own rallies. Sometimes there was violence between the two groups.

In August of 1969 there were riots between Catholics and Protestants in Belfast and in Londonderry, Northern Ireland. After this, England sent in troops to patrol Northern Ireland. Those troops are still there.

The social protesters weren't necessarily involved in the political disputes over the partition of the island. Those disputes were escalating also. During the late 1960s and early 1970s the IRA became very active, particularly in Northern Ireland. In 1970 the IRA split into two groups. The Official IRA dedicated itself to working in political and peaceful ways to unite Ireland. The Provisional IRA dedicated itself to continuing terrorist activities in an attempt to end English influence in Northern Ireland. Partly because of Provisional IRA bombings, shootings, and other terrorism, in 1972 England suspended Northern Ireland's government and took direct control of the country.

Caught in the middle between the fighting Protestant and Catholic groups, the British troops fight back. At right, they chase a Catholic mob and at left, a British soldier uses tear gas to disperse a mob of Protestants. The fighting continues to this day with no peaceful solution in sight.

In recent years there have been many acts of violence. For example, July 21, 1972, became known as "Bloody Friday," when twenty explosions in Belfast, Northern Ireland killed 11 people and injured more than 120 others in a matter of minutes. The explosions had been set off by the Provisional IRA.

People having nothing to do with the problem of a divided Ireland often have been killed. This ongoing violence and terrorism between the Catholics and the Protestants and between the IRA and the British soldiers is a result of what the writer Edgar O'Ballance referred to as Ireland's "Heritage of Hate." Both sides have committed acts of violence and murder. Killing has become a part of daily life.

Since 1969 more than two thousand persons—most of them in Northern Ireland—have been killed in bombings and shootings between the various factions. At least twenty thousand people have been injured. As long as it is divided into two parts there appears to be no permanent peace in sight for the small, beautiful island that already has had so much blood shed on its soil.

Leinster House, the Irish parliament building (above) and the Custom House (below) in Dublin

Chapter 5

GOVERNMENT OF THE REPUBLIC OF IRELAND

Ireland affirms its devotion to the ideal of peace and friendly co-operation amongst nations founded on international justice and morality. . . . All citizens shall, as human persons, be held equal before the law. . . . The State guarantees in its laws to respect, and, as far as practicable, by its laws to defend and vindicate the personal rights of the citizen. . . .

From *Bunreacht na hEireann*
(the Constitution of Ireland)

In the Irish language the Republic of Ireland is called *Éire,* or Erin, both modernizations of the word *Eriu,* which was the name of a Celtic goddess.

The flag of the Republic of Ireland has three colored bands of equal size. Outward from the staff, the colors are green, white, and orange. The green represents Ireland's ancient Celts and the Catholics. The orange represents the Protestant tradition. The white center band symbolizes the hope for peace between these two groups. The flag was introduced by Thomas Meagher in 1848.

The Irish national anthem is called *"Amhran na bhFiann"* in Gaelic—"The Soldier's Song." The harp—an instrument enjoyed by the Irish for centuries—is the nation's official emblem. The shamrock (a three-leaved clover) is the country's national flower.

The Irish Republic's form of government is a parliamentary democracy. It consists of two houses of lawmakers, called the Parliament, or *Oireachtas* in Gaelic. As in any democracy, the people elect most of their lawmakers. The government is based on a constitution that was adopted in 1937.

THE PRESIDENT

The president of the Republic of Ireland is elected for a term of seven years and may serve no more than two terms. The president signs laws, appoints the prime minister and other officials, and is commander of the country's armed forces.

THE PRIME MINISTER

Although the president is called the head of state, the prime minister, called the *taoiseach* in Gaelic, is the country's most important government official and is the head of government. Nominated by the House of Deputies and appointed by the president, the prime minister serves for a maximum five-year term.

The prime minister sees that the country's laws are put into effect. He also selects members of Parliament to head various government departments.

PARLIAMENT (*Oireachtas*)

The Republic of Ireland's Parliament has two main lawmaking bodies. They are called the *Dáil Éireann* (House of Deputies) and the *Seanad Éireann* (Senate).

The House of Deputies is the more important of the two. It

makes the laws for the Republic of Ireland. The 148 House members are elected by the people to five-years terms.

Although only the House can pass laws, the Senate can present bills to the House. Some of the sixty Senate members are appointed by the prime minister and some are elected to five-year terms.

THE COUNTIES AND THEIR GOVERNMENT

The Republic of Ireland is divided into twenty-six counties: Cavan, Donegal, Monaghan, Galway, Leitrim, Mayo, Roscommon, Sligo, Carlow, Dublin, Kildare, Kilkenny, Laoighis, Longford, Louth, Meath, Offaly, Westmeath, Wexford, Wicklow, Clare, Cork, Kerry, Limerick, Tipperary, and Waterford. Councils elected by the people, together with county managers, govern the counties.

It should be added that counties are important socially as well as politically to the Irish. When Irish people meet thousands of miles from Ireland, they may ask one another, "What county are you from?" before inquiring about hometowns. One reason for this is that the Republic of Ireland has few big cities and many small towns. People can more readily identify each other by the well-known county names than by the names of the small towns.

POLITICAL PARTIES AND VOTING

There are three major political parties in the Republic of Ireland. They are the *Fianna Fáil* (Soldiers of Destiny), the *Fine Gael* (the Gaelic People), and the Labour Party. To vote in the Republic of Ireland, a citizen must be eighteen years old.

Dublin, Ireland's most populous city, is divided by the River Liffey. Bridges, such as the Moss Street Bridge above, connect the city.

Chapter 6

THE CITIES OF ÉIRE

Oh, Saint Patrick was a gentleman,
Who came of decent people;
He built a church in Dublin town,
And on it put a steeple.

Old Song

Roughly half of the Republic of Ireland's 3.5 million people live in small farming villages. The other half live in cities or in big towns. The republic has no huge cities. The largest, Dublin, has a population of only 550,000. Cork is the country's only other city with a population exceeding 100,000.

DUBLIN

Nearly two thousand years ago a small settlement stood where the River Liffey empties into the Irish Sea on the Emerald Isle's east coast. This settlement was called *Dubh Linn,* meaning "black pool." The name referred to the dark color of the Liffey at that location. During the 800s, Viking invaders captured the settlement and built it into a city.

Today the River Liffey flows right through the heart of the city, cutting it almost exactly in half. People travel between north and south Dublin across bridges.

St. Patrick's Cathedral (left) and O'Connell Street

Dublin is the Republic of Ireland's most populous and most important city. It is also the nation's capital. The country's lawmakers meet in a large eighteenth-century building called Leinster House.

In Dublin one can walk the same streets that Padraic Pearse and Eamon de Valera traversed when they went into battle during the Easter Rebellion of 1916, or see Dublin Castle, which Robert Emmet tried to capture in 1803. Names of places bring to mind the patriots of old. Pearse Street, Wolfe Tone Quay, and Parnell Square are all named for Irish leaders. The Daniel O'Connell statue on O'Connell Bridge still bears bullet holes made during the Easter Rebellion.

For those who love literature, Dublin is one of the most pleasurable cities on earth. The great writers Jonathan Swift, George Bernard Shaw, John Millington Synge, William Butler Yeats, James Joyce, and Oscar Wilde all were born in or very near

The grounds of Trinity College (left) and the open-air Henry Street market

Dublin. (Playwright George Bernard Shaw's birthplace is on Synge Street; playwright John Millington Synge was born on Shaw Street!)

Among the many historic buildings in Dublin is Christ Church Cathedral, built by a Christianized Viking king nearly a thousand years ago, in 1172. The heart of Dublin's patron saint, Laurence O'Toole, is one of the church's ancient relics. Nearby Saint Patrick's Cathedral was built around 1225. It is said that it was near the site of this church that Saint Patrick struck the ground with his staff, causing a fountain of water to flow. The water was used to baptize converts to Christianity.

In addition to its historical, literary, and political importance, Dublin is the Republic of Ireland's main center for education. Trinity College (also called the University of Dublin) was founded in 1591. Trinity College Library has the country's largest book collection, including the ancient manuscript of the Book of Kells.

Grafton Street (above), the Botanical Gardens (below left), and O'Connell Street (below right) are some of Dublin's attractions.

Brian Boru's harp, the Republic of Ireland's national symbol, is also kept in the Trinity Library. In addition, the National University of Ireland has a college in Dublin. (Other colleges of the National University of Ireland are in Cork and in Galway.)

Among Dublin's museums is the National Museum, where ancient art works can be seen. Two of its famous pieces are the Tara Brooch and the Ardagh Chalice, each twelve hundred years old and made of silver and gold. Another museum, the National Gallery, houses famous paintings.

Dublin's people, who live in a variety of housing, from tenements to mansions, work at a broad range of jobs. The products they make include cloth and clothes, whiskey and stout (a kind of beer), furniture, machines, foods, chemicals, paper, and metals. Dublin is, by far, the Republic of Ireland's most important manufacturing city and is home to more than a third of the country's manufacturing facilities. Many products made in Dublin are shipped to other cities of the world from the city's port.

CORK

Cork is the Republic of Ireland's second largest city and one of the country's prettiest. It is located in the far southern part of the country near the Atlantic Ocean. The center of Cork is an island on the River Lee. The rest of Cork consists of hilly lands north and south of the river.

During the late 500s, Saint Fin Barr built a church and a school where Cork now stands. According to legend, Fin Barr had come to kill Ireland's last dragon. Vikings established Cork as a trading city during the 900s.

River Lee (left) and Cobh, the natural harbor of Cork (right). Father Prout wrote of Cork and its bells. "Wherever I wander, and thus grow fonder, Sweet Cork, of thee; With thy bells of Shandon, That sound so grand on the pleasant waters of the River Lee."

During the long years of English rule, the city earned the nickname "Rebel Cork." Among the Cork patriots who died in Ireland's struggle were two lord mayors—Thomas MacCurtain and Terence MacSwiney.

Cork is known for its beautiful churches. Saint Fin Barr's Protestant Cathedral stands on the spot where the dragon-fighting saint built his church more than fourteen hundred years ago. Saint Anne's Church is famed for the eight bells in its steeple.

A college of the National University of Ireland is located in Cork. The university has a fine collection of *ogham,* a form of lettering found on Celtic tombs.

Foods, cars, and beer are among the products made in Cork. Many products go in and out of the city by ship. Cork has one of the best natural harbors in all of Europe.

Father Prout wrote this song-poem about the Blarney Stone: "There is a stone there, that whoever kisses, Oh! he never misses to grow eloquent. 'Tis he may clamber to a lady's chamber, or become a member of parliament."

Cork also has produced several famous writers. The short-story writers Frank O'Connor and Sean O'Faolain were born in Cork. Another famous Cork writer was Francis Sylvester Mahony, who wrote under the name Father Prout.

The Blarney Stone, a world-famous Irish landmark, can be seen just five miles from Cork. The stone is in the fifteenth-century Blarney Castle. It is below the battlements in the south wall of the castle. According to legend, the castle's owner once saved his home from destruction by sweet-talking the attackers. Anyone who kisses the Blarney Stone, a feat that can be accomplished only by hanging head downward, is supposed to receive the gift of persuasive talk.

To this day, people who try to get their way with flattery are said to be "full of blarney."

Stately homes in Limerick (left) and downtown Killarney (right)

The seaport town of Cobh is near Cork. Once known as Queenstown, Cobh was called "the saddest spot in Ireland" by the English writer H.V. Morton. That is because it once was the main port from which Irish emigrants sailed to North America. Today Cobh is an important fishing town that also has a naval base and a shipyard.

LIMERICK

Located at the mouth of the River Shannon in the southwestern Republic of Ireland, Limerick was founded by Vikings in about the year 900. Today Limerick is the third largest city in the Republic of Ireland—after Dublin and Cork.

Foods and clothes are among the products made in Limerick. Like Dublin and Cork, Limerick is an important port city. From Limerick, ships take products down the River Shannon and out to the Atlantic Ocean. The largest air facility in the Republic of Ireland—Shannon Airport—is near Limerick.

This pub in Kilkenny (left) and these stone houses in Tipperary reflect the life-style found in towns throughout Ireland.

You may have heard of humorous, five-line poems known as limericks. These funny, and sometimes bawdy, poems are named for the city of Limerick, but no one knows exactly why.

KILLARNEY

Killarney, a little town of less than ten thousand people in the southwestern Republic of Ireland, is famed for the beautiful lakes, mountains, and woods nearby. The lovely Lakes of Killarney, with their more than forty islands, are just outside the town. Ruins of ancient churches and castles can be seen on the shores and islands of the lakes. All this scenic beauty has helped make Killarney one of the leading tourist spots in the Republic of Ireland.

A main shopping street in Galway

WATERFORD

Vikings founded Waterford in the early 1000s. Located near the Atlantic Ocean in the southeastern Republic of Ireland, this city of about thirty thousand people is a fishing center and one of the country's main ports. Waterford glass, a very famous and high-quality crystal, is made in the city.

GALWAY

Founded in the 1200s, Galway is located in the western part of the country near Galway Bay. Many old castles, including Aughnanure Castle, Dungory Castle, and Portumna Castle, can be seen in the Galway area. Old Irish customs and the Gaelic language are still very much alive in this region. Galway is also home to a college of the National University of Ireland.

The famous Aran Islands stretch across Galway Bay southwest of Galway. The people of these rocky islands, cut off as they are from the rest of Ireland, have pursued an old-fashioned fishing and farming existence that resembles the way of life of past centuries.

Ireland's towns and cities reflect the nation's ancient and pastoral heritage. Threadneedle Road (above) winds its way to the Atlantic Ocean in Salt Hill, County Galway. The narrow streets of Wexford remind visitors that this town was settled by the Danes in the ninth century. The town of Sligo (below) is in the northwestern part of Ireland. The Benbulben Mountains are in the background.

Once most of the people of Ireland were farmers; today more and more people make their living in towns and cities. But farmers still milk their cows by hand, and family farms, such as this one in County Mayo, remain common sights in rural areas.

Chapter 7

THE PEOPLE AND THEIR WORK

The population of the Republic of Ireland is very young, with more than half the people under twenty-five years of age. The population is also growing. We have to provide job opportunities for that ever-growing number of young people. With increased mechanization in the farming community, the number of people working in agriculture has declined on a continuing basis over the last couple of decades. The best way to create employment for all these young people is through industry and industry-related fields.

An official of the Industrial Development
Authority of Ireland

AGRICULTURE

In days of old, nearly everyone in Ireland raised livestock or grew crops. Although there are other ways of making a living in the Republic of Ireland today, agriculture is still important. About one out of five wage earners makes a living from farming. More than two-thirds of the nation is farmland.

The raising of livestock is the primary agricultural activity. About 90 percent of the farmland is pasture. Beef cattle graze on the rich grasses of the central plain. When they are fat enough, they are sold and eventually wind up on someone's dinner table.

The milk of dairy cattle is used to make butter, cheese, and packaged milk. Pigs, sheep, and horses are among the other livestock raised in the Republic of Ireland.

Only about 10 percent of the farmland is used for growing crops. Barley, wheat, sugar beets, and potatoes are among the crops grown on that land. The first potatoes in Ireland were planted by Sir Walter Raleigh, an Englishman, on land given to him by Queen Elizabeth I.

Today the Republic of Ireland's farmers produce more than enough meat, milk, and other foods to supply the country's inhabitants. Part of their output is exported.

In the 1950s, the Republic of Ireland began a program to assist industrial growth in the country. It did this for several reasons. For one, the country at that time had to import a large amount of the goods needed by its people. This was often more expensive than if those goods had been made within the country. Second, the introduction of labor-saving farm machinery meant fewer people were needed for farming. The growth of industry would mean more jobs. Third, the government recognized that the world was hungry for manufactured goods and was ready to pay for them.

As part of its program for economic expansion, the government in recent years has offered tax relief and other incentives for industries to settle in the country. As a result, the Irish Republic now has one of the fastest-growing industrial sectors in all of Europe. More than 330,000 people—roughly a third of the labor force—are involved in manufacturing.

Although many factories are Irish owned, many others belong to firms in foreign countries, particularly the United States. More than four hundred U.S. companies have factories in the Republic of Ireland. Firms from the United Kingdom, West Germany,

A German-owned chemical factory in County Limerick (left) and worker heating glass at the Cavan Crystal factory (right) represent some of the industries on the island.

Japan, Canada, The Netherlands, and many other countries have also set up factories in the republic.

Located mainly in Dublin and other big cities, the country's factories produce a long list of goods. Cloth, metals, paper, and furniture are among the major products. Food packaging and the making of beer and Irish whiskey are also important industries. In fact, the Guinness Brewery is the largest in Europe. Among other industries are glassware, printing, cement and other construction products, chemicals, drugs, and computers and other electronic equipment. Although the Republic of Ireland still imports more goods than it exports, in recent years the country's exports have been increasing greatly.

One important event in the country's industrial development occurred on January 1, 1973, when the Republic of Ireland became a member of the European Economic Community, formerly known as the Common Market. This is an organization of European nations sharing a number of goals, including the improvement of their economic condition. A great benefit of membership for the Irish Republic is that industrialists who manufacture within the country can export their products duty-free to other member countries. This means that manufacturers can sell products more cheaply—and therefore generate more business—than they could without this membership.

A ride in an old-time jaunting cart is a must for tourists.

Despite the government's efforts, as of early 1984 the unemployment rate in the Republic of Ireland was an extremely high 15 percent. The further growth of industry is one way to relieve the problem of unemployment.

TOURISM

Each year several million people visit the Republic of Ireland—about as many people as actually live there. These visitors make tourism a very important business.

Among the many tourist attractions are lovely landscapes and important historic, religious, and literary sites. The Republic of Ireland has yet another big allure. For millions of people scattered throughout the world, the country is the home of their ancestors.

In the United States there are more than forty million persons—nearly 20 percent of the country's population—of Irish descent. This means that the United States has more than ten times as many people of Irish heritage as does the Republic of Ireland itself. Each year, hundreds of thousands of these Irish-Americans visit the Emerald Isle to seek out their families' villages and meet "long-lost" relatives. A well-known example of a famous

Tinkers, the gypsies of Ireland, once traveled in horse-drawn wagons. Today tourists can rent similar wagons to tour the island. Fish and fishing are becoming important to the country's economy.

American making a trip to Ireland occurred in 1963, when President John F. Kennedy paid a visit. Each year there are many less-publicized visits by Irish-Americans, as well as by people of non-Irish heritage.

All these tourists provide an important boost to the nation's economy. They put money into the pockets of people who operate hotels, pubs, stores, and tourist attractions.

OTHER JOBS

People in the Irish Republic work at many other kinds of jobs besides manufacturing, farming, and tourist businesses. Many people own their own small shops and stores. There are also doctors, lawyers, government workers, construction workers, fishermen, teachers, and people of just about every other occupation you can name.

OVER
CLUB

Chapter 8

THE PEOPLE AND THEIR CULTURE

After resting for a while, Brian dragged his brothers down to the boat and laid them carefully inside, and lying there between life and death the three Sons of Turenn were borne back to Erin. After journeying over the waves for a long time like this, Brian put up his head and looked over the sea to the west.

"I see Ben Eader, Dun Turenn, and Tara of the Kings, my brothers," he said gently to them.

The dying brothers opened their eyes when they heard this, and asked him to raise their heads on his breast so that they might get one last glimpse of the land of Erin. "And then," they said, "we care not whether we live or die after that."

From "The Quest of the Children of Turenn,"
retold by Eileen O'Faolain in her book
Irish Sagas and Folk-tales

Even since the Potato Famine, emigration has cut into the population of the Republic of Ireland. For many years, the population figures continued to decrease. Recently, however, those figures have begun to climb. This rise is due mainly to new industries, which keep people in the country by providing jobs for them. The republic now has the fastest-growing population in western Europe, with more than half the people under the age of twenty-five.

Like people everywhere, the 3.5 million Irish display many individual differences, yet also share many customs and have developed a distinctly Irish culture. That sharing is only natural for a people who also have shared so many hardships for so long. Add to this the fact that Ireland is an island and therefore separate from the European mainland, and you have another reason why the Irish have developed their own distinctive culture.

IRISH NAMES

Many Irish names begin with *Mac, Mc,* or *O'.* MacCool, McCormack, O'Neill, O'Connell, MacNeill, MacDiarmada, MacDermott, MacDonagh, O'Rahilly, O'Toole, MacCurtain, MacSwiney, O'Connor, O'Faolain, O'Casey, O'Leary, O'Flaherty, and O'Callaghan are a few of the Irish names that appear in this book. *Mac* and *Mc* mean "son of" or "descendant of." *O'* means "grandson of" or "descendant of." MacDermott, then, means descendant of Dermott and O'Neill means descendant of Neill.

Ireland was one of the first countries to adopt hereditary surnames. The practice became prevalent about the time of Brian Boru, roughly a thousand years ago.

During the years when England dominated Ireland, many Irish names were anglicized. For example, the name *Mac Giolla Brighde,* meaning "son of the follower of Saint Brigid," became MacBride. *Mac Conmara,* meaning "son of the hound of the sea," became MacNamara. Among the names in use in the Republic of Ireland today are the old Irish names, as well as the anglicized forms of those names.

RELIGION

About 97 percent of the people in the Republic of Ireland are Catholics. Few countries have a larger proportion of people of one religion.

The Catholic church has played a major role in the country's history. Back when the English banned Catholic worship, the Irish knew they were being persecuted as Catholics. But because this persecution was so widespread, they came to feel they were being persecuted as a nation, too. In this way, their religion helped the Irish to view themselves as one people.

Religion is still important in the personal lives of most of the Irish. Almost every city and town has at least one Catholic church, and on Sundays most of the churches are filled. The country's many priests are respected and their opinions are valued. The priests visit the sick, give advice to people regarding their everyday problems, and help in the planning of events such as weddings.

When the Irish take their vacations, they are often pilgrimages to their country's many holy places. For example, each year up to eighty thousand people, many of them barefoot, walk to the top of Croagh Patrick in County Mayo where Saint Patrick spent the forty days of Lent praying and fasting in the year 441. Buses and trains also regularly take people to the monasteries, shrines, and other holy places in the country.

HOMES

In farm regions, many Irish families live much like their ancestors of long ago. The rural areas are still dotted with small houses called cottages whose walls are made of stone or clay. Once these cottages had thatched roofs, but in recent years, many of the cottages have been replaced by new farmhouses and homes.

Many of the people who live in the cottages and farmhouses do without modern conveniences. Heat is often provided by a peat-burning fireplace. Peat, too, may be used for fuel in the cooking stove. In rural areas, many of the people do not have telephones, and some rural cottages still lack electricity, running water, and indoor plumbing.

The people who live in rural areas will tell you there is a good, as well as a bad, side to their life-style. Perhaps they can't call people on the phone, but they tend to spend time visiting friends in person. They may not have large factories in their towns, but they do have clean air and clear blue lakes and rivers.

Life is much different in Dublin and the other cities. There people live much as do residents of other European cities. Some own their own homes, but many live in apartments.

Those who move from the country to the cities find that the urban areas have their good and bad sides, too. Modern heating systems and other conveniences make life easier. But there are overcrowded tenement buildings in the cities, and the air has been polluted by factories.

FAMILY LIFE

Irish people are known for their religious faith, their love for their island, their enjoyment of each other's company, and their close family ties. So important is the idea of family that the constitution "recognises the Family as the natural primary and fundamental unit group of Society, and as a moral institution

Music, whether it is learning to play the pipes or singing the old songs, is a vital part of Irish culture.

possessing inalienable. . . rights. . . . The State, therefore, guarantees to protect the Family. . . as indispensible to the welfare of the Nation. . . . "

Irish families are so close that, until recently, many young women and men remained at home with their parents beyond the age of thirty. This was due, in part, to the scarcity of jobs and farmland; but it was also due to the strong bonds between children and parents. Even today, the average age at which Irish men and women marry is well past twenty-five.

Irish families are known for taking care of all family members. For example, the Irish consider it a sin to put older relatives in old people's homes. Generally the family group expands to include relatives of all ages. An Irish child might live with his or her parents, grandparents, and perhaps an aunt or uncle.

Irish children learn at an early age to value love, loyalty, other people, and their own emotions. Irish legends and songs abound with adults who go to great lengths to help their friends, and with children who spend lifetimes avenging wrongs to their parents. In Irish stories even the mightiest heroes weep openly at the deaths of friends and generally speak what they feel.

Love for their homeland is also instilled in Irish children. The Irish love their country intensely because they had to fight so hard to free it and because so many of their kinfolk had to leave Ireland over the centuries. Irish songs and stories tell of people, such as the three sons of Turenn, who long for one last glimpse of the Emerald Isle before they die.

Although things are changing, most Irish families are run in an old-fashioned way. Tasks are often strictly divided between mothers and fathers, much as in American families of the 1800s.

The mother of the house would cook the Irish stew, bacon and cabbage, potato cakes, and other meals. She would also do the cleaning and would be the parent largely responsible for raising the children. The Irish respect women and even call their country "Mother Ireland," but the women have to do a very large share of the work at home.

An Irish father, after working all day, would probably spend several evening hours at the local pub. Pubs—which are combination taverns and social clubs—are quite popular in Ireland. There the men drink stout, ale, and beer, play darts, and talk with their friends. Until recently, women had to sit in closed booths if they were allowed in the pubs at all.

Not all Irish women stay at home taking care of the house and children. Recently many women, particularly the younger ones, have gone out into the working world. Working women are often grossly underpaid. Because changes occur slowly in the Republic of Ireland, this old-fashioned treatment of women is likely to continue for many years.

EDUCATION

Irish children are required to attend school from the age of six to the age of fifteen. First comes a Primary Education, where students learn reading, writing, arithmetic, and the Irish and English languages. They also spend much time on music, art, crafts, and environmental studies.

Second Level Education is the equivalent of high school. Irish youths have a choice of several kinds of Second Level Education. Some choose to pursue a general course of studies. Others who have decided to become farmers or factory workers can learn the required skills at special vocational schools.

Upon completion of Second Level Education, some students elect to go on to a university or college. Trinity College (also called the University of Dublin), founded in 1591, is the country's oldest university. The National University of Ireland, with its fifteen thousand students and three colleges, is the largest.

The Republic of Ireland also has colleges of education for those who want to become teachers. The Royal College of Surgeons is one of the schools that provide training for doctors. Many budding artists attend the National College of Art and Design in Dublin. There are also colleges for those who want to become farmers, fishermen, musicians, and lawmakers.

THE ARTS

The Irish have excelled at poetry and storytelling for two thousand years. In the days of the Celts and early Christians, poets received royal treatment. For a great verse, a poet might be given a horse or even a piece of land.

The works handed down over the centuries attest to the genius of the ancient poets. Unfortunately, many of the ancient stories are lost forever. In the centuries before there was a written Gaelic language, the tales were told orally. When a written language for

Gaelic was developed, only some of the stories were put into books.

In recent centuries, the Emerald Isle has produced many writers of genius. Jonathan Swift, born in Dublin, was one of the great writers of the 1700s. George Bernard Shaw, James Joyce, John Millington Synge, Sean O'Casey, and William Butler Yeats were great Irish writers. Elizabeth Bowen, Oliver Goldsmith, Frank O'Connor, Sean O'Faolain, Seamus Heaney, Brian Friel, Hugh Leonard, Brian Moore, John Montague, Samuel Beckett, Liam O'Flaherty, Lady Augusta Gregory, Brendan Behan, and Oscar Wilde are a few other well-known Irish writers, past and present. People often find it amazing that a nation half the size of Illinois has produced so many important writers. Certainly one reason is that in past centuries, when the Irish had so many of their freedoms taken from them, they turned to storytelling as a way to express their feelings, thoughts, and even their very sense of self.

Although particularly famous for literature, the Irish have excelled at other art forms. Wonderful examples of sculpture, painting, and the other pictorial arts can be seen throughout the country. Many beautifully decorated stones, such as the ones at Newgrange, have been found in Stone Age graves. Early Celtic pillars and stones, such as the Turoe Stone, can also be seen. Throughout the Irish countryside, beautifully carved Celtic crosses are stone monuments made by Irish artists more than a thousand years ago.

In recent times, Ireland has produced a number of talented painters. One of the most famous was Jack Yeats, the brother of writer William Butler Yeats. Other well-known Irish artists include portrait painter John Butler Yeats (the father of William Butler and Jack), Estella Solomon, and John Keating.

Ireland has a long musical heritage. The country has its own national folk dances, including the Irish jig. Irish folk songs, sung to the accompaniment of harp, fiddle, or flute, are lovely. The songs tell of Irish heroes, lost loves, and the people's love for their homeland.

THE WEARING OF THE GREEN (A street ballad)

This song was sung throughout Ireland after 1798

O Paddy dear, and did you hear the news that's going round,
The shamrock is forbid by law to grow on Irish ground;
And Saint Patrick's day no more we'll keep, his color can't be seen,
For there's a bloody law against the wearin' of the green.
I met with Napper Tandy and he took me by the hand,
And he said, "How's poor ould Ireland and how does she stand?"
"She's the most distressful country that ever you have seen,
They're hanging men and women there for wearin' of the green."

Then since the color we must wear is England's cruel red;
Sure Ireland's sons will ne'er forget the blood that they have shed;
You may take the shamrock from your hat and cast it on the sod,
But 'twill take root and flourish still, tho' underfoot 'tis trod.
When the law can stop the blades of grass from growing as they grow,
And when the leaves in summertime their verdure dare not show,
Then I will change the color I wear in my corbeen,
But till that day, plase God, I'll stick to wearin' of the green.

But if at last our color should be torn from Ireland's heart,
Her sons with shame and sorrow from the dear ould soil will part;
I've heard whisper of a country that lies far beyant the say,
Where rich and poor stand equal in the light of freedom's day.
O Erin must we leave you, driven by the tyrant's hand,
Must we ask a mother's welcome from a strange but happier land?
Where the cruel cross of England's thraldom never shall be seen,
And where, thank God, we'll live and die, still wearin' of the green.

John McCormack (left) was an international opera star.
Irish flute makers (right) continue an ancient craft.

For the performance of more formal music, Ireland's cities have opera houses and concert halls. During the early 1900s John McCormack, born in Athlone, Ireland, became one of the most famous opera and concert singers in the world.

The Republic of Ireland has a practical way of assisting its creative people. Writers, composers, painters, and sculptors of any nationality who live in the republic do not have to pay taxes on earnings from their works—if their work is accepted by the revenue commissioners as having "artistic or cultural merit."

CRAFTS

Kept in poverty as they were by the English, the Irish *had* to learn to make items for their own daily use. Today some Irish handicrafts are so well known that they are highly prized in other lands.

The weaving of wool is one of Ireland's best-known crafts. The women of the Aran Islands have long been famous for knitting beautiful woolen sweaters. Originally each family on the islands had its own distinctive sweater pattern so that fishermen who drowned could be identified by their sweaters. Wool knitters can be found throughout the Republic of Ireland today.

The making of glassware has been important for many years. Beautiful Waterford glass was made in the city of Waterford from the late 1700s until 1851. One hundred years later in 1951, the Waterford factory reopened and resumed making its fine crystal. Cavan and Galway are two other cities where glassware is made.

In days of old, Ireland had no furniture stores. Woodworkers chopped down trees and then used the wood to build tables and chairs. Woodworkers who make furniture can still be found, particularly in the counties of Leitrim, Clare, and Limerick. The making of leather goods, baskets, jewelry, musical instruments, and candles are other Irish crafts.

GAMES AND SPORTS

One day nearly a thousand years ago, Brian Boru's son was playing chess with another man. A third person offered advice that cost Brian's son the game. There was an argument that led to an armed battle. Ireland's chess players still take the game seriously, although not quite *that* seriously. Darts, bingo, and bridge are among the other games popular in the country today.

In days of old, Cuchulainn was reputed to have won a hurling match by himself against a team of twelve. Hurling, still a very popular sport, is similar to field hockey. Each side has fifteen players. Using sticks, the players try to knock a small leather ball

A boys' hurling team from Ennis Island (left) and the Killarney races

through their opponents' goalposts. Hurling matches are held between various country teams, with the season culminating in the All-Ireland Hurling Championship each September in Dublin. Crowds of up to eighty thousand attend the finals, which are as exciting to the Irish as the World Series is to Americans. There is also a women's version of hurling, called *camogie*.

Gaelic football and road bowling are two other ancient Irish sports. Gaelic football, still extremely popular, combines aspects of rugby and soccer. Road bowling is really a kind of race. Using metal balls, the bowlers see who can complete a two- or three-mile course in the least number of throws. Expert bowlers can roll the ball more than six hundred feet at a time.

Horse racing is one of the Republic of Ireland's most popular sports. There are more than two dozen race tracks in the country. The Irish Derby, held each June in Kildare, and the Irish Grand National, held near Dublin during Easter week, are the country's most famous races. Greyhound dog racing is also popular. The dogs are raced on tracks, and, in some places, across open fields. Other popular sports include boating, golfing, swimming, fishing, horseback riding, bicycling, jogging, and boxing.

Several Irish athletes have won Olympic gold medals for their country. In both 1928 and 1932 Patrick O'Callaghan won the gold in the sixteen-pound hammer throw. In 1956 the runner Ron Delany won the gold medal in the 1,500-meter race. Another great Irish athlete, Eamonn Coghlan, set a world record for the indoor mile run in 1981 with a time of 3:50.6.

LANGUAGE

The first Irish people spoke a language that remains unknown today. The Celts brought the Emerald Isle its first known language—Gaelic. Often called Irish, Gaelic was the country's main language for more than two thousand years.

Among other things, the English outlawed the speaking of Gaelic. Because of this, the English language became dominant. By 1850 less than a quarter of the Irish spoke Gaelic.

During the late 1800s, while the Irish were fighting to free their country and make it an independent nation again, patriots tried to revive all aspects of Irish culture. This included the ancient Gaelic language, stories, and sports. In 1893 Douglas Hyde and Eoin MacNeill founded the Gaelic League to restore Ireland's language. They were only partly successful. Although at the turn of the century Irish poets were writing in Gaelic and children in thirteen hundred schools were learning the language, Gaelic never did reclaim its position as the national language.

Today, only about one fourth of the people in the Republic of Ireland know Gaelic well enough to use it in daily conversation, and only about fifty thousand people actually use it as their main language. The Irish-speaking areas are known as the *Gaeltacht*. Nearly every Irish person can speak English, the country's predominant language. The Irish have a beautiful accent, called a brogue, when they speak English.

In the Republic of Ireland signs are written in English and Gaelic. George Bernard Shaw was credited with saying that although it was true that most Irish couldn't read Gaelic, the language was used because the Irish knew that the English couldn't read Gaelic either.

SOME COMMON GAELIC WORDS

máthar: mother
athar: father
deirfiúr: sister
dearthár: brother
sean-athair: grandmother
sean máthair: grandfather
ainte: aunt
oncal: uncle
colceathar: cousin
bricfeást: breakfast
lón: lunch
dinéar: dinner
cistin: kitchen
leithreas: bathroom
seomra fáiltithe: living room
scian: knife
forc: fork
spúnóg: spoon
uibheacha: eggs
prataí: potatoes
feoil: meat
bainne: milk
caifé: coffee
beoir: beer
úl: apple
buachall: boy
cailín: girl
fear: man
bean: woman
sea: yes
nih-ea: no
deas: right
clé: left
scoil: school
obair sa bhaile: homework
eaglais: church
múinteoir: teacher
doctúir: doctor
banaltra: nurse
aturnae: lawyer
sagart: priest
ceann: head
lámh: hand
géag: arm
cos: leg
méar: fingers
méar-coise: toes
gluaisteán: automobile
eitleán: airplane
clog: clock
leaba: bed
codladh sámh: good-night

DAYS OF THE WEEK IN GAELIC

Luan: Monday
Mairt: Tuesday
Céadaoin: Wednesday
Déardaoin: Thursday
Aoine: Friday
Sathairn: Saturday
Domhnach: Sunday

MONTHS IN GAELIC

Eanar: January
Feabhra: February
Márta: March
Aibreán: April
Bealtaine: May
Meitheamh: June
Iúl: July
Lúnasa: August
Mean Fomhair: September
Deire Fomhair: October
Mí naSamhna: November
Mí naNollag: December

NUMBERS

Aon: One	Aon Déag: Eleven
Dó: Two	Dó Dhéag: Twelve
Trí: Three	Tri Déag: Thirteen
Ceathar: Four	Ceathar Déag: Fourteen
Cúig: Five	Cúig Déag: Fifteen
Sé: Six	Sé Déag: Sixteen
Seacht: Seven	Seacht Déag: Seventeen
Ocht: Eight	Ocht Déag: Eighteen
Nací: Nine	Naoí Déag: Nineteen
Deich: Ten	Fichead: Twenty

IRISH BLESSINGS

May the road rise to meet you. May the wind be always at your back. May the sun shine warm upon your face, the rains fall soft upon your fields, and, until we meet again, may God hold you in the palm of his hand.

May you be in heaven a half hour before the devil knows you're dead.

IRISH SAYINGS

In the world of the blind the one-eyed man is king.

A full cabin is better than an empty castle.

He who has water and peat on his farm has the world.

Don't desert the highway for the short cut.

Often a person's mouth has broken his nose.

You can't find a thing except in the place it is.

A blessing does not fill the belly.

The people go, but the hills remain.

May the saints preserve us.

Hope protects the oppressed.

A shut mouth catches no flies.

SOME TRADITIONAL IRISH RECIPES

Irish stew: Mutton, onions, potatoes, parsley, thyme, salt, and pepper are main ingredients

Sweet potted herrings: Made with onions and spices in addition to the herrings

Potato soup: Made with onions, carrots, and lots of potatoes

Carrageen moss jelly: A jelly made with Carrageen, an edible seaweed often washed up on Ireland's western shore in April and May

Bacon and cabbage: A tasty and traditional dish. (Corned beef and cabbage is the American version of this dish.)

Potato cakes: One of many ways the Irish prepare potatoes

Barm brack: A kind of fruit-filled, syrup-topped cake traditionally made at Halloween

Spiced apple tarts: A pastry filled with apples, dates, cinnamon, and sugar

Dublin coddle: A stew made with bacon, sausages, onions, and potatoes

Chapter 9

THEIR FAME LIVES ON

We find a country where for 1500 years... as far back as historic knowledge can reach, one national force has overshadowed and dominated all others... the power of a great literary tradition.

Alice Stopford Green, *Irish National Tradition*

Thousands of Irish people are world famous in various fields of endeavor. There were the Irish saints, including Saint Ciaran, Saint Patrick, Saint Enda, Saint Brigid, Saint Brendan, Saint Columcille, Saint Kevin, and Saint Laurence O'Toole. There have been the many great writers, artists, and musicians. There have been scientists, including Robert Boyle, who studied the expansion and compression of gases. Among Irish inventors was John Philip Holland, the person primarily credited with inventing the submarine. The country's great architects include James Hoban, designer of the White House in the United States. It is remarkable that so small a country should have produced so many noteworthy individuals. Here are short biographies of just a few of the many famous Irish people.

SAINT BRIGID (BORN CIRCA 453, DIED CIRCA 524)

Brigid was born in what is now County Louth, Ireland. Her father was king of that region. Her mother was a Christian slave who belonged to the king. Like her mother, Brigid was a Christian.

Brigid loved to hear her mother, who ran a dairy, tell stories of how Saint Patrick was at that very time spreading Christianity to the far corners of Ireland. As a child, Brigid decided that she, too, would build churches and spread the Christian faith.

Brigid's father loved but couldn't understand her. Once Brigid gave his jeweled sword to a poor man on the road. "I'm a Christian and Christians should give," Brigid explained to the king. Another time Brigid's father announced that she was to marry a grand poet. He was shocked when she refused, declaring that she was going to dedicate herself to her religion. Soon after that Brigid left home.

Among Brigid's friends were several young women who were also Christians. Brigid and her friends found a lovely spot where a giant oak stood above the River Liffey. They gathered branches and built huts for their living quarters. Then they built a larger hut to be their church. Because their settlement stood near the big oak, it was called the Church of the Oak.

Young women and men from all over Ireland heard about Brigid's settlement and went there to become priests and nuns in the community. The huts had to be replaced by larger buildings to accommodate the new arrivals. One building became a convent for nuns. Another was a monastery, where the monks lived.

Each person had a task in the religious community. Those who were skilled at crafts made clothes and farm tools. Others farmed, cooked, tended livestock, or created illuminated manuscripts. Priests and scholars who came to visit marveled at the beautiful manuscripts created at the Church of the Oak.

Brigid began to travel to far-off places in Ireland. She spoke with other young women and men who wanted to become nuns and monks, and she founded other convents and monasteries.

St. Brigid

People told so many stories about Brigid that today it is difficult to separate fact from fiction. For example, it was said that because animals sensed Brigid's kindness, she was able to tame a wolf and teach it tricks. Wild geese and ducks were said to fly down from the sky at her call.

When Saint Brigid died, she was buried next to Saint Patrick at Downpatrick Cathedral, in what is now Northern Ireland. It is said that at Kildare, a town that grew up around the Church of the Oak, a fire was kept burning for a thousand years in memory of Saint Brigid.

JONATHAN SWIFT (1667-1745)

Jonathan Swift was born in Dublin. Because he was a Protestant and his ancestors were English, he always considered himself English. Yet Swift spent most of his life in Ireland and wrote a great deal about the country.

By the age of three, Jonathan could read the Bible, but at Kilkenny School, and later at Trinity College, he wasn't much of a student. He preferred reading poetry and history on his own to doing schoolwork. On his twenty-first birthday, Jonathan got in trouble for insulting a college official. He was to spend the rest of his life hurling words at people and institutions he didn't like.

Jonathan Swift

After working for a decade as secretary to a statesman in England, Jonathan Swift became pastor of a church in Laracor, County Meath, Ireland. From 1713 until his death thirty-two years later, Swift was dean of Dublin's Saint Patrick's Cathedral. During those years Swift wrote some of the greatest works in the English language.

Jonathan Swift was saddened and angered by the plight of the Irish people. He wrote essays describing English cruelty and distributed them throughout the countryside. In a famous essay called "A Modest Proposal," Swift suggested that the problem of hunger in Ireland could be solved if people were to kill and eat the children! Of course he didn't mean that. He was trying to show just how desperate the situation had become in Ireland.

Swift was a satirist—a writer who criticizes people and society by poking fun at them. In *A Tale of a Tub* he makes fun of the religious and learned people of his time. In *The Battle of the Books* he describes a fight between ancient and modern books to determine which are better. Swift makes it clear that he favors the older books.

Gulliver's Travels is Jonathan Swift's most famous work. It tells of the voyages of Lemuel Gulliver, a ship's doctor. Among the strange beings Gulliver meets are the tiny Lilliputians and the giant Brobdingnagians. Here is Swift's description of Gulliver's first encounter with the Lilliputians after he awakens and finds himself shipwrecked on a beach:

> In a little time I felt something alive moving on my left leg, which advancing gently forward over my breast, came almost up to my chin; when, bending my eyes downwards as much as I could, I perceived it to be a human creature not six inches high, with a bow and arrow in his hands, and a quiver at his back. In the mean time, I felt at least forty more of the same kind (as I conjectured) following the first. I was in the utmost astonishment, and roared so loud, that they all ran back in a fright; and some of them, as I was afterwards told, were hurt with the falls they got by leaping from my sides upon the ground. . . .

Although *Gulliver's Travels* can be enjoyed as a children's adventure story, adults also enjoy it for its satire about human nature. Jonathan Swift is considered the greatest satirist in the literature of the English language.

GEORGE BERNARD SHAW (1856-1950)

Like Jonathan Swift, George Bernard Shaw was born in Dublin of English parents. Shaw spent only the first twenty years of his long life in Ireland. But, unlike Swift, Shaw considered himself an Irishman. He once wrote: "I write as an Irishman. . . full of instinctive pity for those of my fellow creatures who are only English."

George Bernard Shaw

As a young man, Shaw couldn't decide what career to pursue. He liked art, but couldn't draw. He liked music, but lacked musical talent. At fourteen he had to quit school. He went to work as an office boy—a job he despised.

At the age of twenty, Shaw left Ireland and went to London, where his failures continued for a time. He wrote five novels that no one would publish. Then he began to win the interest and admiration of the public as a music and theater critic. He also began to write successful plays.

Shaw always presented important ideas in his plays. *Arms and the Man* is an antiwar play. *Pygmalion* points out the ridiculousness of considering one group of people better than another. With each new play, Shaw's fame grew. When he was sixty-seven years old, he wrote *Saint Joan*—his great play about the young French girl who was burned at the stake in 1431 and declared a saint nearly five centuries later. In this play, Shaw showed how remarkable people are often rejected during their own lifetimes. In the last line of the play, Joan of Arc states this herself: "O God that madest this beautiful earth, when will it be ready to receive Thy saints? How long, O Lord, how long?"

When Shaw was ninety-four years old, he fell while working in his garden and died several weeks later. The author of more than fifty plays, George Bernard Shaw is remembered as one of the greatest playwrights since William Shakespeare.

WILLIAM BUTLER YEATS (1865-1939)

William Butler Yeats, who was born in Dublin, spent much of his youth in the town of Sligo in northwestern Ireland. William studied art for a time, but it was his brother Jack Yeats who became a famous artist. After discovering that he had talent as a writer, William Butler Yeats turned to writing poems and plays.

Yeats loved Irish myths, history, and language. These all found their way into his work. He wrote about Cuchulainn and other figures from Irish mythology. He wrote about real Irish leaders, including Maud Gonne, an Irish revolutionary whom he loved. The rhythms of Irish speech can be heard in his complex poems. Here is a portion of "Easter 1916," Yeat's famous poetic tribute to the leaders of the Easter Rebellion:

> We know their dream; enough
> To know they dreamed and are dead;
> And what if excess of love
> Bewildered them till they died?
> I write it out in a verse—
> MacDonagh and MacBride
> And Connolly and Pearse
> Now and in time to be,
> Wherever green is worn,
> Are changed, changed utterly:
> A terrible beauty is born.

William Butler Yeats (far left) and James Joyce

William Butler Yeats is remembered as one of the greatest poets of the twentieth century. He also helped found Dublin's Abbey Theatre, which presented the works of John Millington Synge, Sean O'Casey, and other Irish playwrights.

JAMES JOYCE (1882-1941)

James Joyce was born in Dublin. He was one of seventeen children, only ten of whom lived past infancy. The Joyce family was so poor that they had to move from place to place because they couldn't pay their rent.

James Joyce became a writer, but for years he received no recognition and had to earn his living at other jobs. He wrote book reviews, taught school, and worked in a bank. All the while, he continued to write stories and novels in his spare time.

James Joyce's *A Portrait of the Artist as a Young Man*, published in 1916, is his novel about a young writer. It wasn't until 1922, however, that Joyce achieved fame with the publication of *Ulysses*, one of this century's greatest novels. In this and other works Joyce uses a method of writing called stream of consciousness. He shows the readers his characters' thoughts, making those characters seem like real, living people.

Despite the fame that *Ulysses* brought him, James Joyce continued to have troubles. Some of that trouble came from censorship battles. Because of its language, *Ulysses* was banned for years in many countries. Joyce also had to undergo more than twenty operations for an eye disease that at times left him blind.

Through it all, James Joyce continued to create. So involved was he in his book *Finnegans Wake* that he rewrote it more than a dozen times. Today James Joyce is considered by many to be the greatest novelist of this century.

EAMON DE VALERA (1882-1975)

Edward de Valera, as he was first named, was born in New York City. Edward's mother was Irish and his father Spanish. When Edward was almost three his father died. The boy was sent to Ireland where he grew up on a farm in County Limerick.

Edward learned Gaelic from his grandmother, who told him tales of Finn MacCool and other legendary heroes. At school Edward moved to the top of his class. On the sports field he starred at Gaelic football and hurling. At home he milked the cows, tended the goats, and did other farm chores.

Edward's love for reading became well known in his town. He would sit down by the side of the road on his way home from school to finish an interesting book. He read at the dairy while waiting to make his family's milk delivery. He was also a good listener. At night he listened to relatives and friends talking about England's harsh treatment of the Irish.

Although most boys in those days went into farm work at an

early age, Edward's family sent him to high school and then to college. He became a teacher and was appointed Professor of Mathematics and Physics at Rockwell College in County Tipperary. Later he taught mathematics, French, and Latin at various other schools and colleges. De Valera appeared headed for a quiet life as a college professor.

Because he was interested in the revival of Irish culture, de Valera joined the Gaelic League in 1908. He fell in love with and married an Irish actress, who had changed her name from Janie O'Flanagan to the Gaelic version, Sinead ni Fhlannagain. Edward, too, decided to change his first name to Gaelic. He became Eamon instead of Edward.

Eamon de Valera came to feel that it wasn't enough just to revive Irish literature and language. Ireland, he decided, must be completely free of England. He joined the Irish Republican Brotherhood, walked out of his classroom, got a gun, and prepared to fight in the Easter Rebellion of 1916.

On April 24 de Valera marched 130 armed men through the streets of Dublin. When gunfire broke out, de Valera was in the thick of the battle.

The English put down the rebellion and took Pearse, de Valera, and the other leaders as prisoners. The fact that de Valera had been born in America helped save him from being executed along with Pearse and the others. He was sentenced to life in prison, but as part of the peace negotiations, de Valera and other political prisoners were released.

Crowds welcomed de Valera upon his return to Ireland. First a scholar, then a fighter, now he began a third life—that of a politician. For years he worked to achieve by peaceful means what he had tried to do with his gun in 1916.

Eamon de Valera in 1971

First he was elected to represent County Clare in the English Parliament. In 1917 the Irish elected him president of the Irish Executive Committee for a country that existed in name only rather than in fact. De Valera was unwavering in his desire to make Irish independence a reality. His efforts helped the Irish Free State be recognized by England in 1921. After 1937 he served three times as prime minister, from 1937 to 1948, from 1951 to 1954, and from 1957 to 1959.

In 1949 de Valera helped Ireland totally separate itself from England. He was elected president of Ireland in 1959 and 1973, when he was past the age of ninety. Eamon de Valera stands out as one of the greatest in Ireland's considerable gallery of patriots.

Chapter 10

THE LEGEND OF FINN MACCOOL

"I care not though I were to live but one day and one night, if only my fame and my deeds live after me."

The motto of Cuchulainn, mythological Irish hero

The legends and myths of a people tell a great deal about the history, culture, and traditions of that people. Ireland's ancient stories tell of wars, beheadings, doomed lovers, and enchanted creatures such as leprechauns. Even the funniest Irish stories often have tragic events in them, probably because Irish history itself is so tragic.

FINN MACCOOL AND THE STOLEN CHILDREN

Finn MacCool, the second great hero of ancient Ireland, was supposed to have lived in Ireland in the third century A.D. or thereabouts.

Not only was Finn a great hunter and warrior, he was also a man of thought. As a young man, Finn went off to study poetry with a wise man named Finnegas, who lived on the shore of the River Boyne. For seven years Finnegas had been fishing for the Salmon of Knowledge. It was said that whoever ate this fish would gain great wisdom.

Finn had been studying under Finnegas for a short while when the old man caught the fish. "Cook it for me, MacCool, but don't eat even the tiniest bit of the fish," ordered Finnegas, who of course wanted the wisdom for himself.

It happened that Finn burned his finger on the fish while cooking it. Placing his burned finger in his mouth to soothe the pain, Finn chanced to swallow a tiny bit of the fish. When Finn created a lovely poem on the spot, Finnegas knew that the young man had obtained the salmon's great wisdom.

"It was an honest mistake," said Finnegas. "And it's better for you to have the wisdom than for it to be swimming in the river. Good-bye, Finn," he added, sending his pupil out into the world.

Finn became leader of the Fianna. Although all the warriors were strong and wise, Finn was by far the strongest and wisest. The story of how Finn saved three children from a wicked witch shows how this great hero could use his head to solve problems.

One day Finn was walking by the seaside when a giant came up to him. "The king of the giants needs your help," the huge being said. "A witch has stolen his first two sons and the queen is expecting another child soon. Will you come guard the new child?" Of course, Finn agreed.

On the way to the castle, Finn met a group of wee folk who were playing hurley. "Good day," Finn said to the little people, each of whom was but a few inches high. "Please introduce yourselves."

"I am Hearing Ear," said the first little man. "I can hear things as far away as Scotland."

"I'm called Climber," said the second. "I can climb the walls of the highest castle."

"I'm Knowing Man," said the third. "I can tell the future."

Mist shrouds the mountains of Connemara in County Galway.

There were five others. Finn met Bowman, who could strike a bumblebee with an arrow at a hundred yards. Next came Three Sticks, who could build anything out of wood. Then there was Lazy Back, who couldn't be moved by even the strongest man in the world once he had sat down. Taking Easy told Finn that he could steal anything without being caught. Far Feeler claimed that he could feel a spider crawling along the ground many miles away.

Finn told the wee folk about the witch and the stolen children and asked the little people to help him. Then he asked Three Sticks, "Could you build a ship for me?" Three Sticks made the ship in no time, and they all set out for the kingdom of the giants.

They reached the castle just after the third child had been born. "My little friends and I will guard the child," promised Finn.

That night the eight small men and Finn played chess to pass the time. Shortly after midnight, Knowing Man said, "The witch is about to leave her castle!"

"I hear her getting close—she's here!" said Hearing Ear.

The giant witch stuck her long, gnarled hand down the chimney and tried to snatch the baby. "Lazy Back, sit on her hand!"

Ruins of Dunluce Castle in Northern Ireland

ordered Finn. With Lazy Back sitting on her fingertips, the witch couldn't move her arm. She tried so hard to get her arm away that it was pulled right out of the socket. Still, the clever witch fooled Finn and his eight little friends. She stuck her other hand down the chimney and plucked the child from its crib.

"We'd best run away!" cried the eight little men, fearing that the king would chop off their eight little heads.

"Run we won't!" answered Finn. "We'll follow the witch and rescue the baby and the two other children as well."

They boarded their ship and sailed about for a while until Far Feeler said, "I feel her wickedness nearby!"

They found the witch's castle, but its walls were quite steep. "Now your talents are needed!" Finn told Climber. "Put Taking Easy on your back and climb the castle wall."

With Taking Easy holding on to his neck, Climber scaled the wall. The two little men went in through a castle window. Taking Easy found the baby and picked him up without a noise. He handed the baby to Climber, who carried him down. Then Taking

Kilkenny Castle

Easy found the king and queen's other two sons. Climber took the two children down to Finn and then carried Taking Easy down, too.

The little people and Finn weren't gone long with the three children when the witch began to chase them. "Far Feeler, tell us when you feel her wickedness nearby," said Finn. "And you, Bowman, get your best arrows ready, please."

"She's near!" said Far Feeler.

"Not yet! Wait!" Finn told Bowman. Then "Shoot!" he ordered.

Bowman's arrow pierced the one eye that sat in the middle of the witch's forehead and the evil witch fell dead. Finn and the wee men then sailed back with the three children.

The king and queen were overjoyed. To reward Finn, they loaded the ship with jewels and other treasures, which, of course, Finn shared with his eight little friends.

Finn MacCool had many other adventures—some happy, some sad. Finn fell in love with a beautiful girl named Sava and they married. Sava gave birth to Finn's son, Oisin, a great poet. Unfortunately, though, Sava was turned into a deer by an evil wizard while Finn was out in battle.

Atlantic
Ocean
NORTHERN IRELAND
IRELAND
(EIRE)
Irish Sea
St. George's Channel
North Channel
Belfast
Londonderry
Dublin (Baile Átha Cliath)
Dun Laoghaire
Cork
Cobh
Limerick
Waterford
Galway
Sligo
Wexford
Kilkenny
Tralee
Killarney
Ennis
Athlone
Drogheda
Dundalk
Armagh
Newry
Coleraine
Omagh
Enniskillen
Strabane
Ballymena
Larne
Lisburn
Portadown
Bangor
Dungannon
Downpatrick
Carlow
Clonmel
Tipperary
Mallow
Dungarvan
Arklow
Wicklow
Bray
Tullamore
Mullingar
Longford
Roscommon
Castlebar
Westport
Ballina
Donegal
Letterkenny
Tuam
Ballinasloe
Portlaoise
Thurles
Enniscorthy
Rosslare
Kinsale
Bantry
Skibbereen
Youghal
Achill
Aran Islands
Valencia
Malin Head
Mizen Head
Carnsore Point
Slieve Donard 2796
Carrauntuohill 3414
Macgillycuddy's Reeks
Mourne Mts.
Wicklow Mts.
Sperrin Mts.
Blue Stack Mts.
Galtymore 3018
Lugnaquillia Mtn. 3039
Shannon Airport
Isle of Man
Campbeltown
Stranraer
St. David's
Milford Haven
©Rand McNally & Co. R.L. 83-S-141
Lambert Conformal Conic Projection
SCALE 1 : 2,000,000 1 Inch = 32 Statute Miles
Statute Miles 5 0 5 10 20 30 40 50
Kilometers 5 0 5 10 20 30 40 50 60

Ireland Map Index

MINI-FACTS AT A GLANCE

GENERAL INFORMATION

Official Name: *Poblacht na h-Éireann* (Republic of Ireland)

Other Names: Éire, Erin

Capital: Dublin

Official Languages: Gaelic (Irish), English. Although Gaelic is the first official language, English is the predominant language. Both Gaelic and English are used in all official documents and are taught in the schools.

Government: The Republic of Ireland is a parliamentary democracy. The president is the head of state and is first citizen of the country. He appoints a *Taoiseach* (prime minister), who is the head of government. The *Oreachtas* (Parliament) consists of two bodies—the *Dáil* (House of Deputies) and the *Seanad* (Senate). The members of the *Dáil* are elected directly by the people. The voting age is eighteen. The current government of the Republic of Ireland is based on the constitution of 1937.

Flag: The flag consists of three colored bands of equal size. Green represents Ireland's ancient Celts and the Catholics. Orange represents the Protestants and the Protestant king William III (also known as William of Orange). The white band in the center symbolizes the hope for peace between the two groups.

Coat of Arms: The coat of arms features an Irish harp on a shield.

National Song: *"Amhran na bhFiann"* ("The Soldier's Song")

Religion: Although there is no official church, at least 95 percent of the population is Catholic. Other religions include Church of Ireland, Methodist, and Presbyterian.

Money: The basic unit is the Irish pound (*punt*). There are 100 pence in a pound. Coins are 1/2, 1, 2, 5, 10, and 50 pence. Notes are 1, 5, 10, 20, 50, and 100 pounds.

Weights and Measures: Ireland uses the metric system.

Population: 3,440,427 (April 5, 1981 census)

Provinces: The Republic of Ireland is divided into four provinces, each of which is further divided into counties for a total of twenty-six counties.

Leinster	1,790,521
Munster	998,315
Connaught	424,410
Ulster	230,159

Cities About half the population live in cities or large towns; the other half, in rural areas. The cities listed here are the largest cities in the Republic of Ireland. The figures include suburbs or environs.

Greater Dublin (includes Dún Laoghaire—54,596)	915,115
Cork	149,792
Limerick	75,520
Galway	41,861
Waterford	39,636

(Population figures based on 1981 census)

GEOGRAPHY

Area: 27,136 sq. mi. (70,282 km^2)

Greatest Distances: North to south—289 mi. (465 km)
East to west—177 mi. (285 km)

Highest Point: Carrauntouhill, 3,414 ft. (1041 m)

Lowest Point: Sea level, along the coasts

Land Regions: Seacoasts, mountain ranges, and a central plain

Islands: The Republic of Ireland occupies five-sixths of the island of Ireland and includes the Aran Islands, the Valentia Islands, and Achill Island.

Rivers: The River Shannon is the longest river. It is about 240 mi. (386 km) long. The River Liffey is 75 mi. (121 km) long. Other rivers include the Boyne, the Moy, the Nore, the Suir, the Barrow, the Blackwater, and the Lee.

Mountains: The principal mountain ranges are the Wicklow Mountains, Macgillicuddy's Reeks (Kerry), Knockmealdown and Comeragh mountains (Waterford), and the Twelve Pins (Connemara).

Lakes: Ireland is dotted with lakes. The most beautiful of these are the Lakes of Killarney—the Lower Lake, Muckross Lake, and the Upper Lake—in County Kerry.

Climate: The climate of the Republic of Ireland is mild. Summer temperatures average about 60° F. (16° C) Winter temperatures average about 40° F. (4° C) Snow is rare, except in some mountain areas. The mountains receive about 60 in. (152 cm) of rainfall per year; the central plain receives about 36 in. (91 cm).

NATURE

Trees: Although there were once many types of trees growing in large forests, much of the land was cleared for farms. Today only 5 percent of the land is forest. The government is planting trees to increase the size of the forests. Three species predominate—Sitka spruce, shore pine, and Norway spruce. Most forests are located in Cork, Wicklow, Galway, Tipperary, Waterford, Donegal, Fermanagh, and Derry.

Animals: Ireland has only a few wild animals, including foxes, badgers, otters, red deer, and Irish hare.

Fish: Fish common to the area include herring, cod, mackerel, salmon, periwinkles, lobsters, plaice, rays, and whiting.

EVERYDAY LIFE

Food: Typical foods include Irish stew, spiced beef, bacon and cabbage, potato soup, potato cakes, sweet potted herring, and Dublin coddle. Popular beverages include tea, Irish coffee, Irish whiskey, and beer or stout.

Homes: In cities or towns, families live in houses made of brick or concrete or in apartment buildings. In rural areas, modern houses are replacing traditional stone or clay thatched-roof cottages. Peat is often used as a fuel for both heating and cooking.

What People Do for a Living: About 21 percent of the work force are employed in agriculture, forestry, and fishing. About 32 percent work in industry—manufacturing, mining, etc. The remaining 47 percent are engaged in service occupations—government, education, health, utilities, transportation, etc.

Holidays:

January 1, New Year's Day
March 17, St. Patrick's Day
Good Friday
Easter
Easter Monday
First Monday in June, Bank Holiday
First Monday in August, Bank Holiday
December 25, Christmas
December 26, St. Stephen's Day

Customs: The Irish are very religious. Most people attend church regularly and many make pilgrimages to shrines and other holy places. People marry late in life, partly because of the economy but also because of close family ties. Irish families are very traditional: The women clean, cook, and raise the children; the men work only outside the home. The Irish believe in the extended family; grandparents or other relatives often live with the nuclear family.

Culture: The famous Abbey Theatre in Dublin is popular for its plays. The National Museum contains many ancient Irish treasures; the National Gallery and the National Portrait Gallery contain beautiful works of art. The Arts Council, which was established in 1951, assists the arts and artists by way of grants, scholarships, and awards.

Recreation: Irish families enjoy one another's company and the company of their friends and neighbors. Families often watch television together in the evenings. Men enjoy visiting local pubs, where they drink, talk, and play darts. Participation and spectator sports are popular.

Sports: Hurling is Ireland's leading sport. Other popular sports include Gaelic football, road bowling, boating, golfing, swimming, fishing, horseback riding, bicycling, jogging, boxing, cricket, sailing, and tennis. The Irish also enjoy horse racing and greyhound dog racing.

Health: The Irish are healthy people. The average life expectancy of the women is about seventy-three. For men it is about sixty-nine. Health services are administered by local health authorities under the supervision of the minister of health. The entire population is entitled to some services without charge: school health examinations, child welfare clinics, and treatment of tuberculosis and infectious diseases. Otherwise the cost of public health services is based on the individual's ability to pay.

Communications: There are seven daily newspapers—five in Dublin and two in Cork, including four morning papers that are distributed nationally, and five national Sunday papers. The government owns the radio and television stations, the telephone company, and the telegraph service. People must pay an annual fee to own a television set.

Transportation: Ireland has more than 500,000 licensed road vehicles, about 70 percent of which are private cars, an average of 122 cars per 1,000 population. The extent of the road system is 57,684 mi. (92,829 km), 9,988 mi. (16,071 km) of which are main roads. There is no longer any commercial traffic on Irish canals. The Royal, one of the two major canals, is closed to all navigation; the Grand Canal is maintained in a navigable condition. The major seaports are Dublin, Waterford, Cork, Dún Laoghaire, Rosslare, Limerick, Galway, and Drogheda. International airports are located at Shannon, Dublin, and Cork.

Schools: Education is compulsory from ages six to fifteen. Students in the primary school learn to read and write both Gaelic and English. Other subjects include arithmetic, music, art, crafts, and environmental studies. Students attend a National School until the age of twelve, at which point they transfer to a post-primary school. The secondary schools are similar to high schools in the United States. Although most secondary schools are private, they are supported by the government. Students completing secondary school take the Intermediate Certificate at age fifteen or sixteen and may proceed to a two-year course leading to the Leaving Certificate. Those successful in prescribed areas of the Leaving Certificate examination are qualified for entrance to the two universities—the National University of Ireland (Dublin, Galway, Cork) and the University of Dublin (also called Trinity College).

Principal Products:
Agriculture: Wheat, oats, barley, potatoes, sugar beets, hay, silage
Livestock: Cattle, sheep, pigs, chickens
Fishing: Cod, mackerel, plaice, salmon, sea trout, eels, shellfish
Mining: Peat, lead, zinc, copper, silver

IMPORTANT DATES

6000 B.C.—Human settlement may have begun in Ireland

6000-2000—Stone Age tomb builders and farmers

700—Bronze Age

400 B.C.—Celts arrive in Ireland

A.D. 432—St. Patrick arrives in Ireland. Beginning of golden age in Ireland

400—O'Neill family begin rule in Ulster

795—Vikings invade Ireland

1002—Brian Boru becomes the first Christian high king

1014—Vikings defeated. Brian Boru killed in his tent

1160s—Turlough O'Connor overthrows Dermot MacMurrough

1171—Henry II gains control of Ireland

1541—Henry VIII becomes king of Ireland

1560—Queen Elizabeth becomes English ruler

1591—Trinity College founded

1601—Hugh O'Neill fights Queen Elizabeth

1600s—James I forces Irish Catholics to leave Northern Ireland

1641—Irish revolt against England

1649—Irish defeated by Oliver Cromwell

1685—James II, a Catholic, becomes king of Ireland

1688—James II forced to give up the throne

1690—Battle of the Boyne

1695-1725—Penal Laws enacted against Catholics

1798—Theobald Wolfe Tone's rebellion against English rule

1801—Act of Union makes Ireland part of the United Kingdom of Great Britain and Ireland

1803—Robert Emmet's revolt

1823-1843—Daniel O'Connell fights for and wins rights for Irish Catholics

1829—Irish granted right to hold office

1845-1847—Potato Famine

1858—Fenian Movement founded

1867—The Fenian Movement revolt

1877-1891—Charles Stewart Parnell is major political force in Ireland. He heads Irish Party and fights for Irish Home Rule

1886—Home rule bill defeated

1892—Home rule bill defeated

1893—Gaelic League founded, part of a cultural revival that increases Irish nationalism

1904—Abbey Theatre founded

1905—Sinn Fein political organization founded

1914—Home rule bill passed

1914-1918—World War I

1916—Easter Rebellion

1919—House of Deputies declares Ireland an independent republic

1920—Government of Ireland Act divides Ireland into two separate political units

1921—Irish Free State founded

1922—Civil War in Ireland begins

1926—Eamon de Valera founds Fianna Fail, fights against 1922 treaty with England

1932—De Valera breaks political and economic ties with England

1937—The constitution adopted, declares Irish sovereignty

1939-1945—World War II

1949—Ireland declared an independent republic

1955—Ireland joins the United Nations

1964 to present—Street fights, bombings, and executions continue in Northern Ireland. All attempts to end fighting, share power or form stable government of both Catholic and Protestant interests fail

1973—Ireland joins the European Common Market

1976—Laws passed to increase punishment for terrorism

IMPORTANT PEOPLE

Sara Allgood, (1883-1950), actress, born in Dublin

Michael Balfe, (1808-1870), composer, born in Dublin

Samuel Beckett, (1906-), playwright who won the Nobel Prize in Literature in 1969, born in Fotrock, a suburb of Dublin

Brendan Behan, (1923-1964), playwright, born in Dublin

George Berkeley, (1685-1753), philosopher, born in Kilkenny

Brian Boru, (926-1014), king of Ireland born near Killaloe, County Clare

Robert Boyle, (1627-1691), physicist who developed Boyle's Law, born in Lismore

St. Brigid (453-524), born in County Lowth

John Bagnell Bury, (1861-1927), classical scholar, born in County Monaghan

Michael Collins, (1890-1922), Irish leader, born in County Cork

Padraic Colum, (1881-1972), playwright, born in Longford

St. Columcille (Columba) (521-597), born in Donegal

St. Columban (540-616), born in Leinster

James Connolly, (1870-1916), leader of the Easter Rebellion, born in Ulster

William T. Cosgrave, (1880-1965), statesman, born in Dublin

Michael Davitt, (1846-1906), founder of Irish Land League, born in Straide, County Mayo

Eamon De Valera, (1882-1975), first president of the Irish Republic, born Edward de Valera in New York City

Dudley Digges, (1879-1947), actor, born in Dublin

Gerard Dillon, (1916-), artist, born in Belfast

Robert Emmet, (1778-1803), Irish patriot, born in Dublin

John Field, (1782-1837), composer, born in Dublin

Barry Fitzgerald, (1888-1961), actor, born William Shields in Dublin

Edward Fitzgerald, (1763-1798), statesman, born in Dublin

Oliver Gogarty, (1878-1957), poet, born in Dublin

Oliver Goldsmith, (1728-1774), author, born in Pallas, County Longford

Henry Graltan, (1746-1820), statesman, born in Dublin

Lady Augusta Gregory, (1852-1932), author, playwright, founded the Abbey Theatre, born in Rovborough, County Galway

Arthur Griffith, (1872-1922), journalist, who published *The United Irishman,* born in Dublin

William Rown Hamilton, (1805-1865), astronomer, born in Dublin

Edward Hincks, (1792-1866), discoverer of the lost Sumerian language

Douglas Hyde, (1860-1949), founder of the Gaelic League and first president of the Irish Republic, born in Castlerea, County Roscommon

James Joyce, (1892-1941), author, born in Dublin

Sean MacBride, (1904-), winner of Nobel Peace Prize in 1974, born in Paris of Irish parents

John McCormack, (1884-1945), opera singer, born in Athlone

Siobhan McKenna, (1923-), actress, born in Belfast

Thomas Meagher, (1823-1867), introduced the Irish flag, born in Waterford

George Augustus Moore, (1852-1933), author, born in County Mayo

Thomas Moore, (1779-1852), composer and poet, born in Dublin

Edna O'Brien, (1930-), author, born in Tuamgraney, County Clare

Sean O'Casey, (1880-1964), playwright, born John O'Casey in Dublin

Frank O'Connor, (1903-1966), author, born Michael O'Donovan in County Cork

Turlough O'Connor, (1088-1156), king of Connaught

Sean O'Faolain, (1900-), author, born John Whelan in County Cork

Liam O'Flaherty, (1896-), author, born on the Aran Islands

Sir William Oripen, (1878-1931), artist, born in Stillorgan

Laurence O'Toole, (1130-1180), patron saint of Dublin, born in Dublin

Charles Stewart Parnell, (1846-1891), fought for home rule, born in Avondale, County Wicklaw

St. Patrick (c. 389-c. 461), brought Christianity to Ireland, born in England

Padraic Pearse, (1879-1916), fought in Easter Rebellion, born in Dublin

Lennox Robinson, (1886-1958), playwright, born in Douglas, County Cork

George Russell, (1867-1935), poet who used the letters "AE" as his pen name, born in Lurgan, County Armagh

George Bernard Shaw, (1856-1950), playwright, born in Dublin

Richard Brinsley Sheridan, (1751-1816), playwright, born in Dublin

James Stephens, (1882-1950), poet, born in Dublin

Jonathan Swift, (1667-1745), author of *Gulliver's Travels* and other satires, born in Dublin

John Millington Synge, (1871-1909), playwright, born in Rathfarnham near Dublin

Theobald Wolfe Tone, (1763-1798), founded United Irishmen, born in Dublin

Ernest Walton, (1903-), scientist who won Nobel Prize in physics in 1951, born in Dungarvan, Waterford

Oscar Wilde, (1854-1900), playwright, born in Dublin

Jack Butler Yeats, (1871-1957), artist, born in London and grew up in Sligo

John Butler Yeats, (1839-1922), artist, born in Tullyish, County Down

William Butler Yeats, (1865-1939), author, poet, playwright, founded the Abbey Theatre, born in Dublin

INDEX

Page numbers that appear in boldface type indicate illustrations

About the Author

Dennis Fradin attended Northwestern University on a partial creative writing scholarship and graduated in 1967. He has published stories and articles in such places as *Ingenue, The Saturday Evening Post, Scholastic, Chicago, Oui,* and *National Humane Review.* His previous books include the Young People's Stories of Our States series and the Disaster series for Childrens Press. *Bad Luck Tony* was published by Prentice-Hall. He is married and the father of three children.